I0496226

This
Book
Belongs
To

WWW.TATTOOWOO.COM

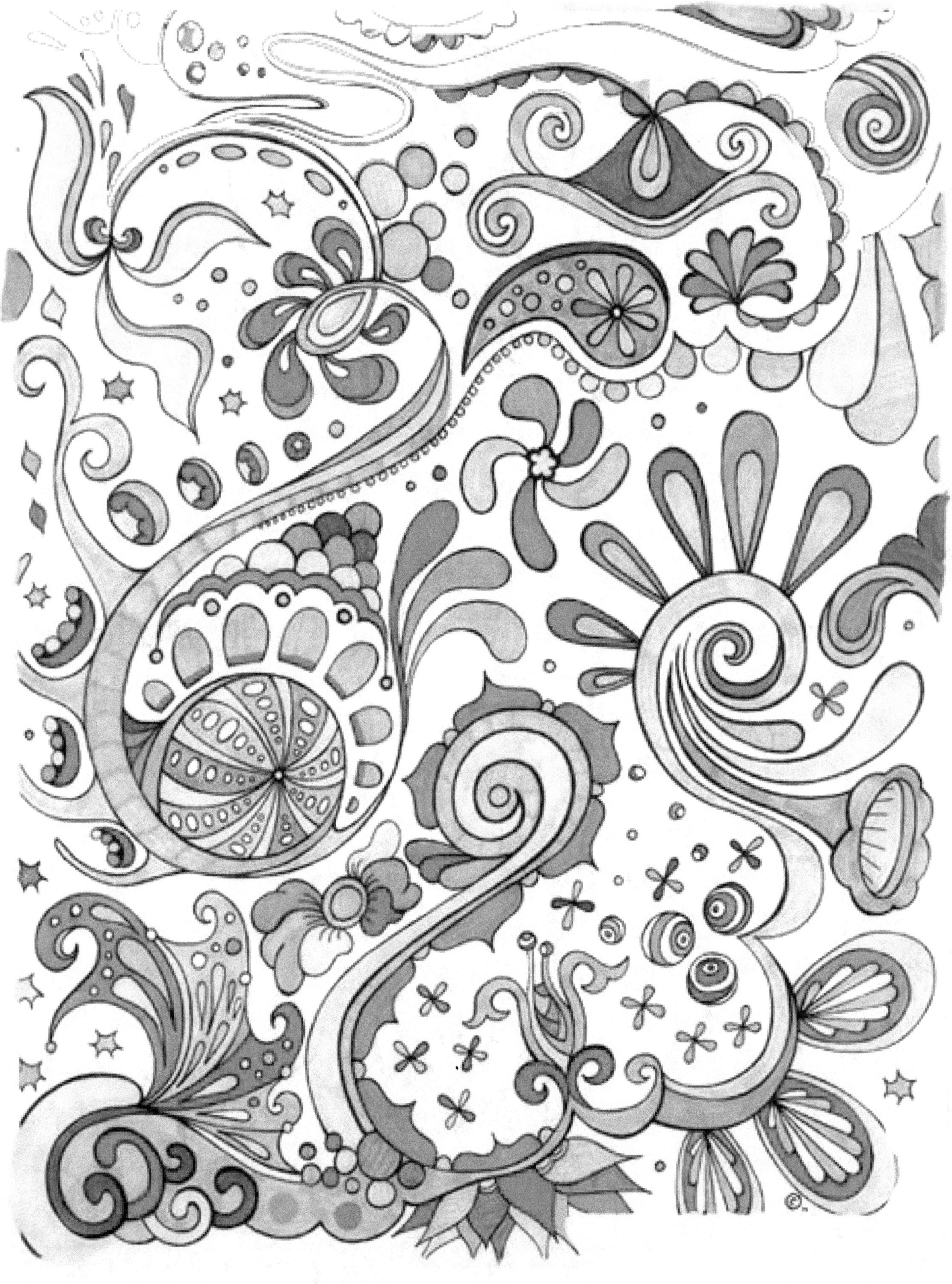

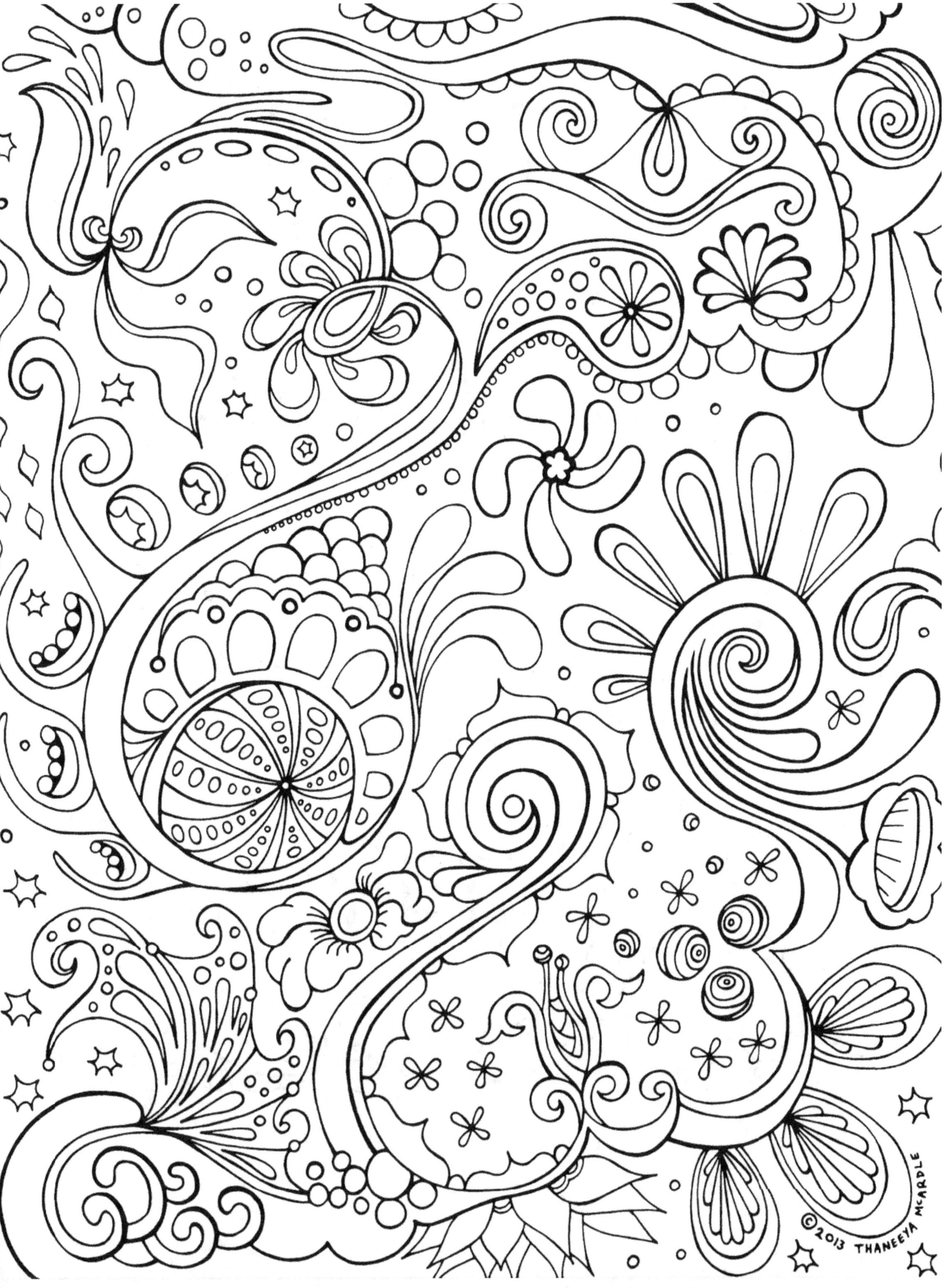
©2013 THANEEYA McARDLE

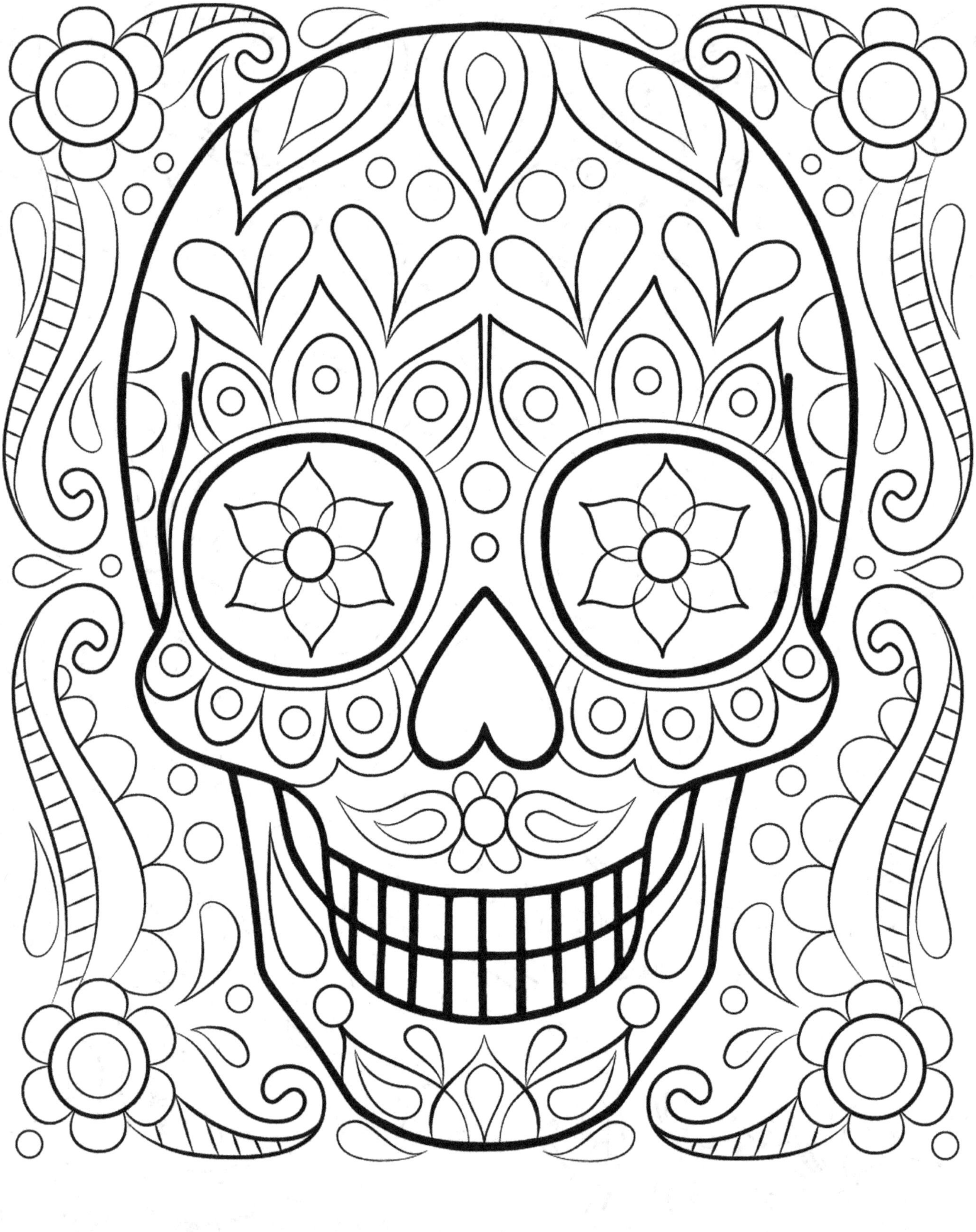

Ch s

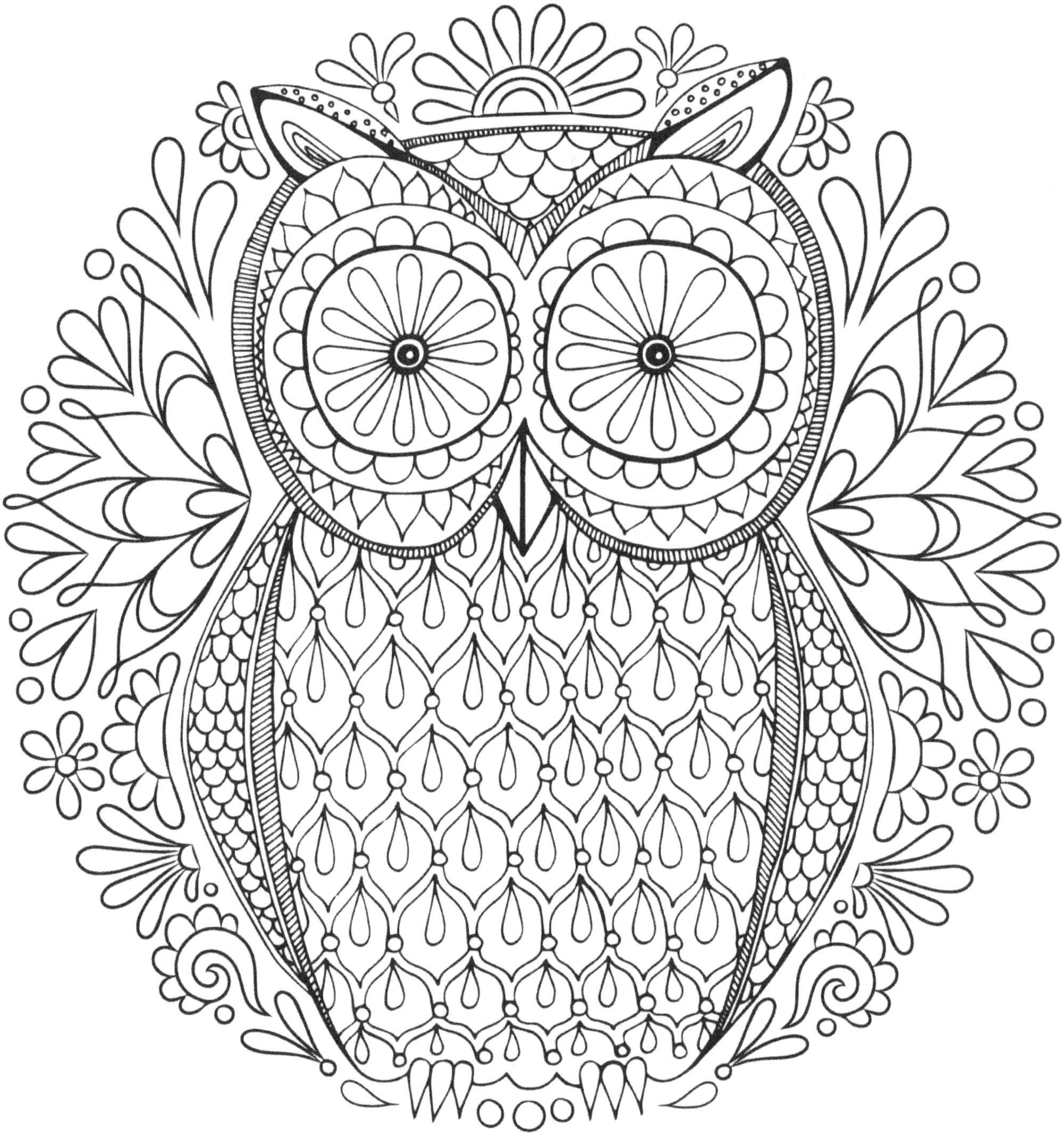

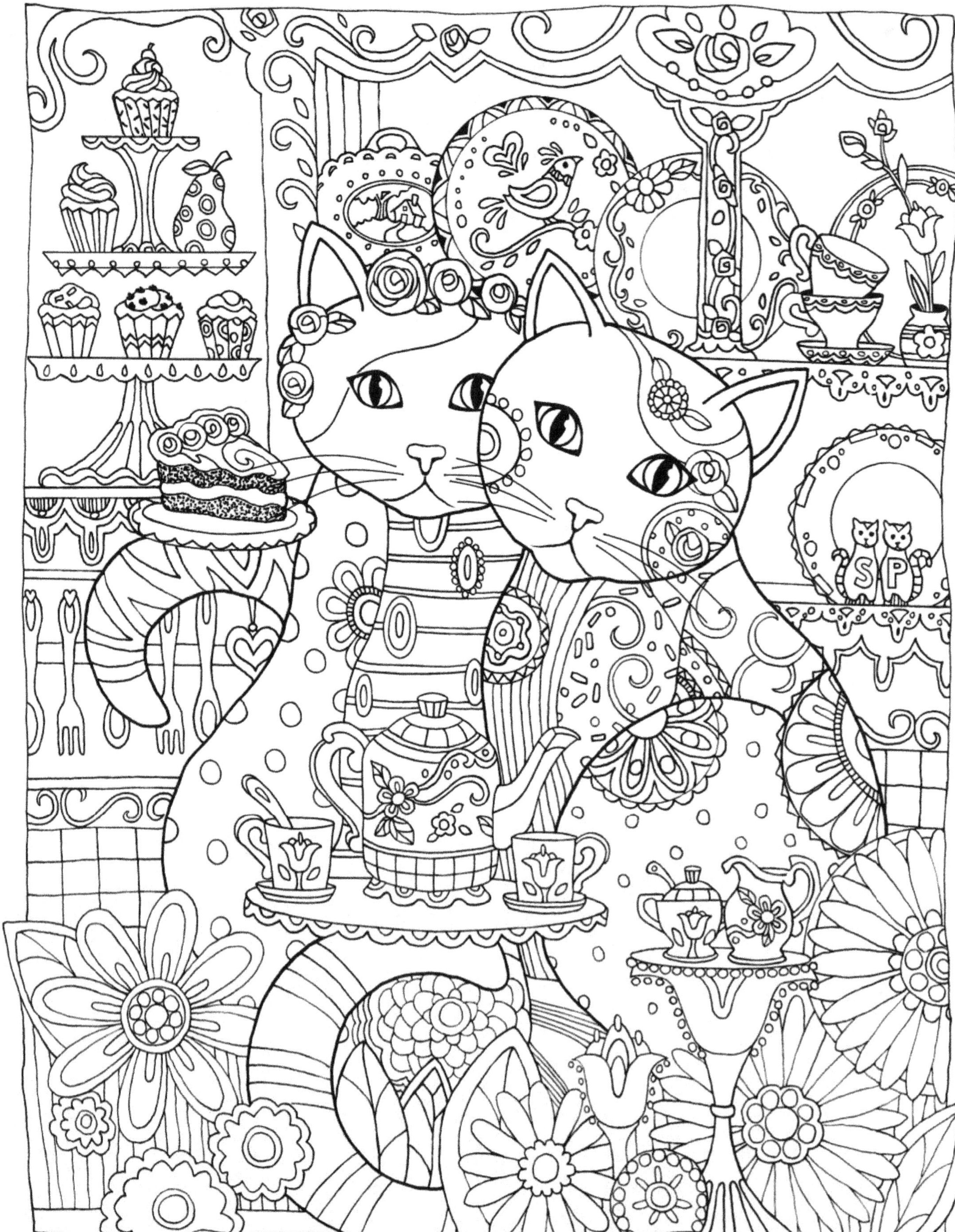
SP

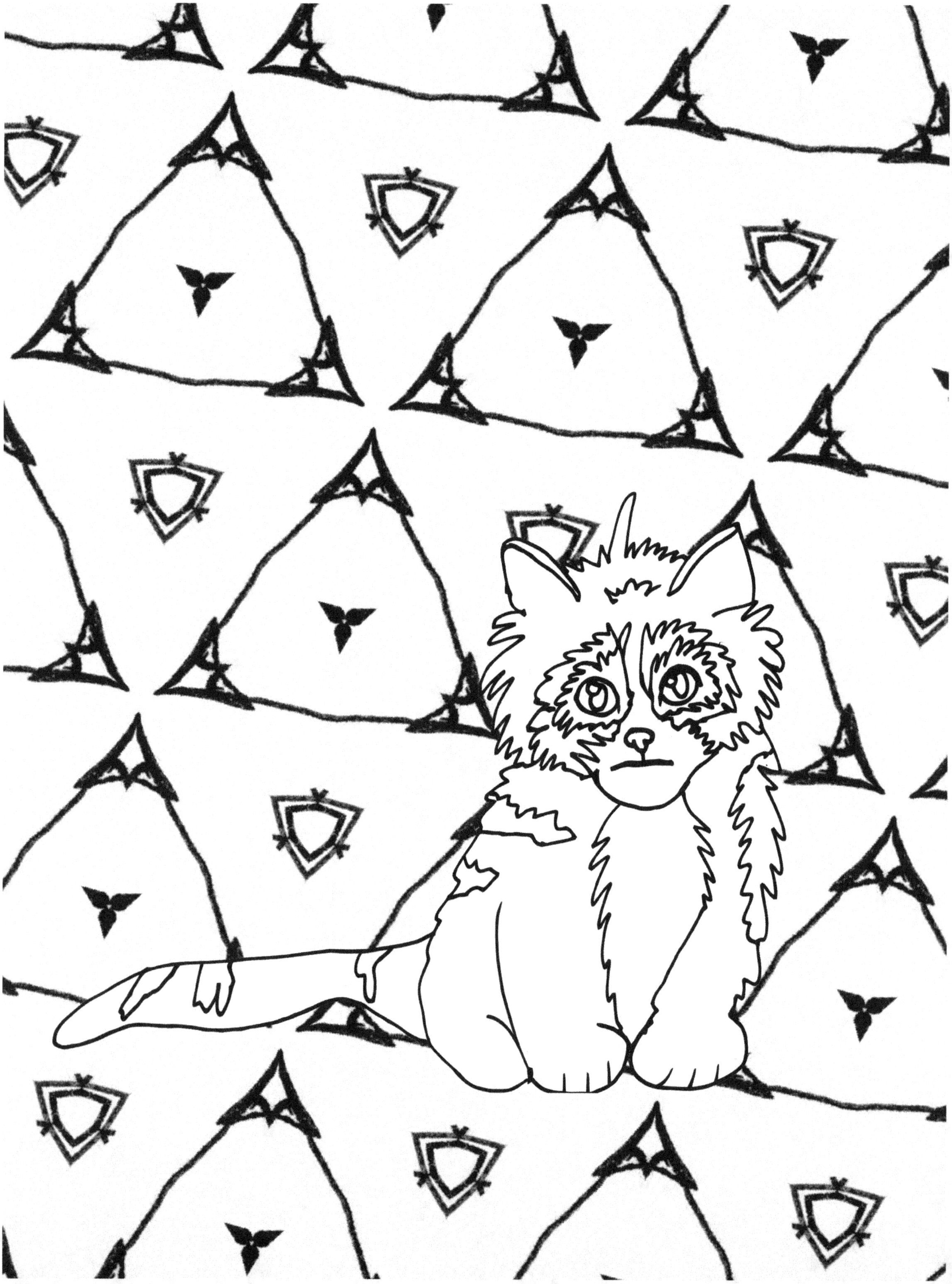

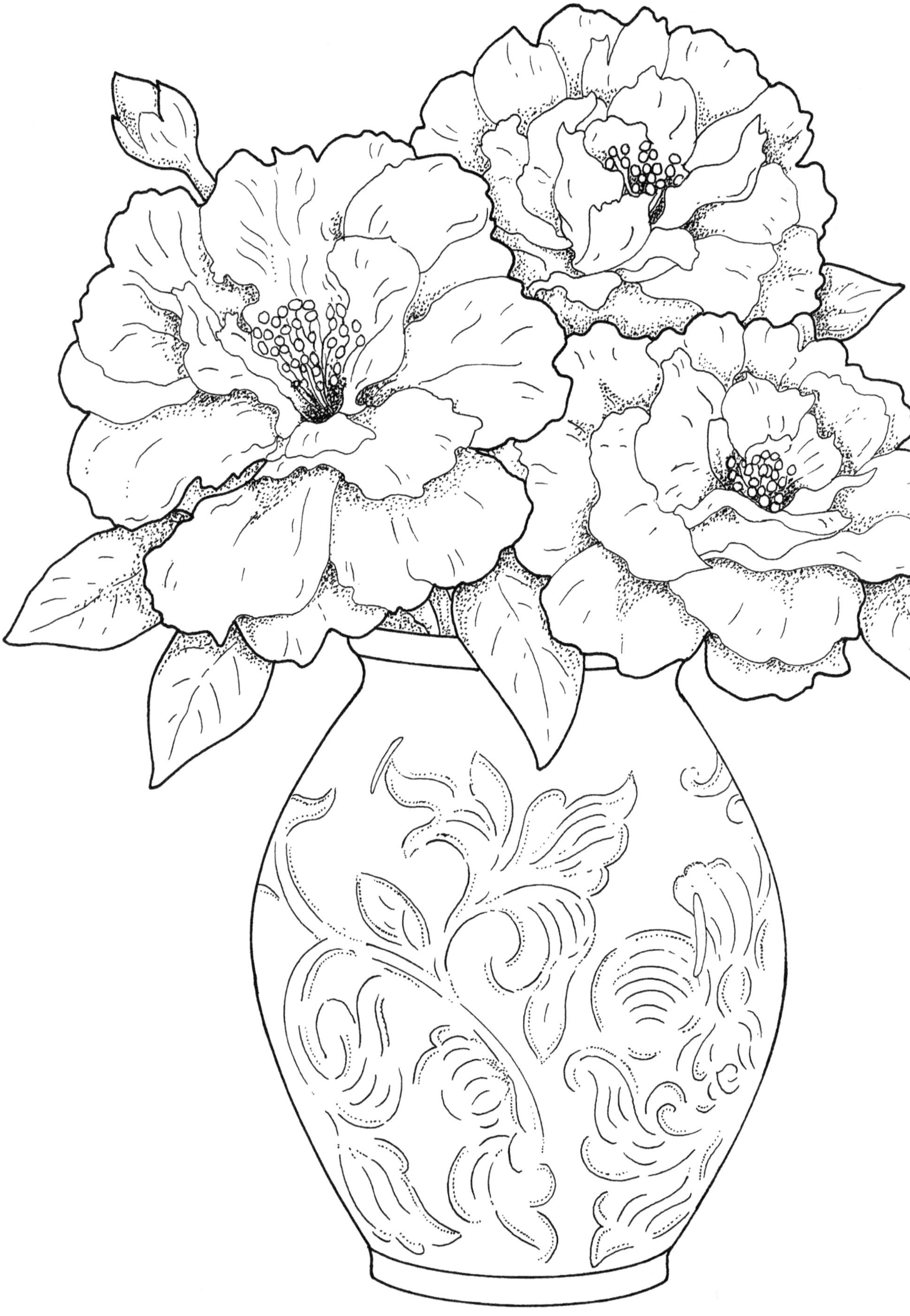

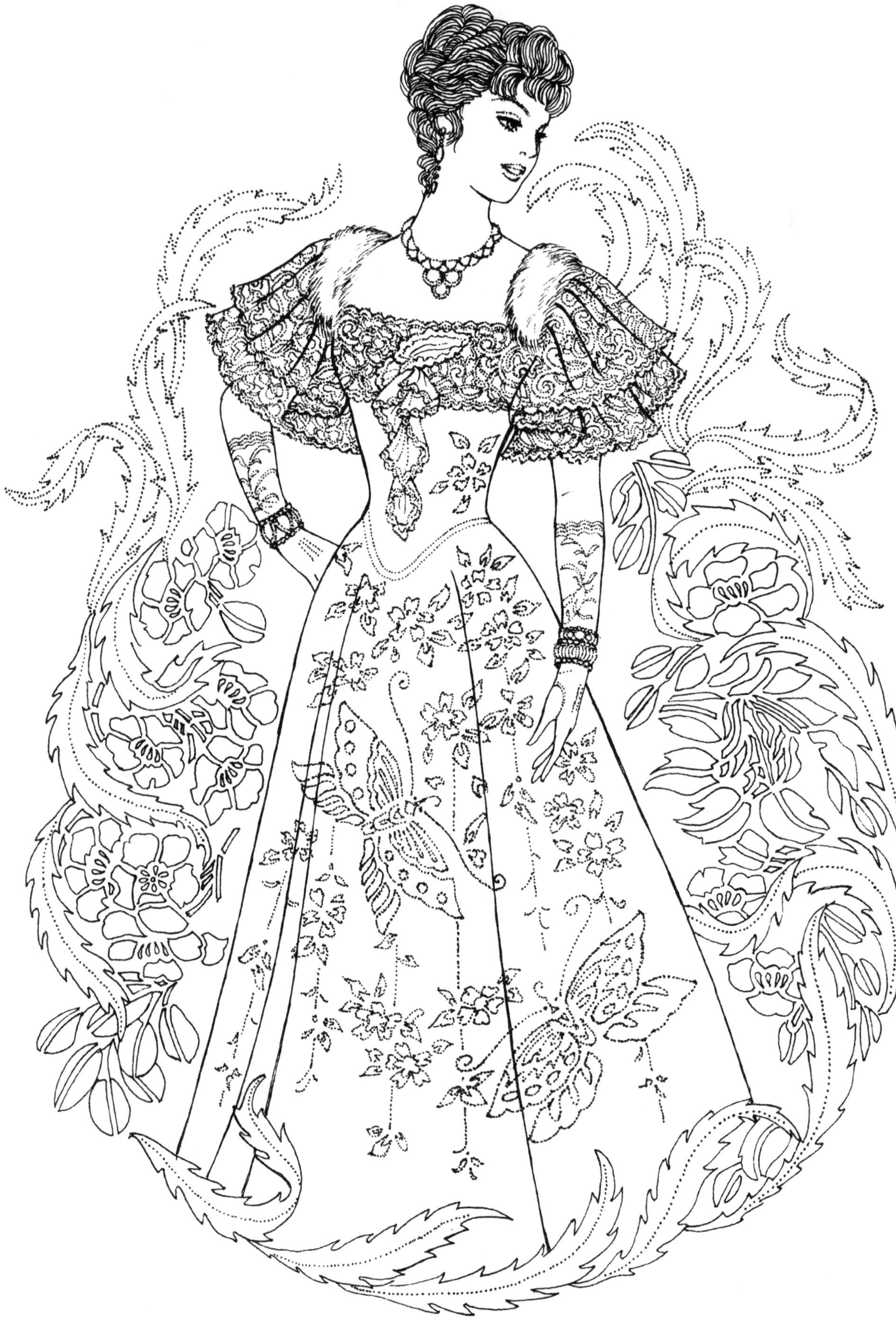

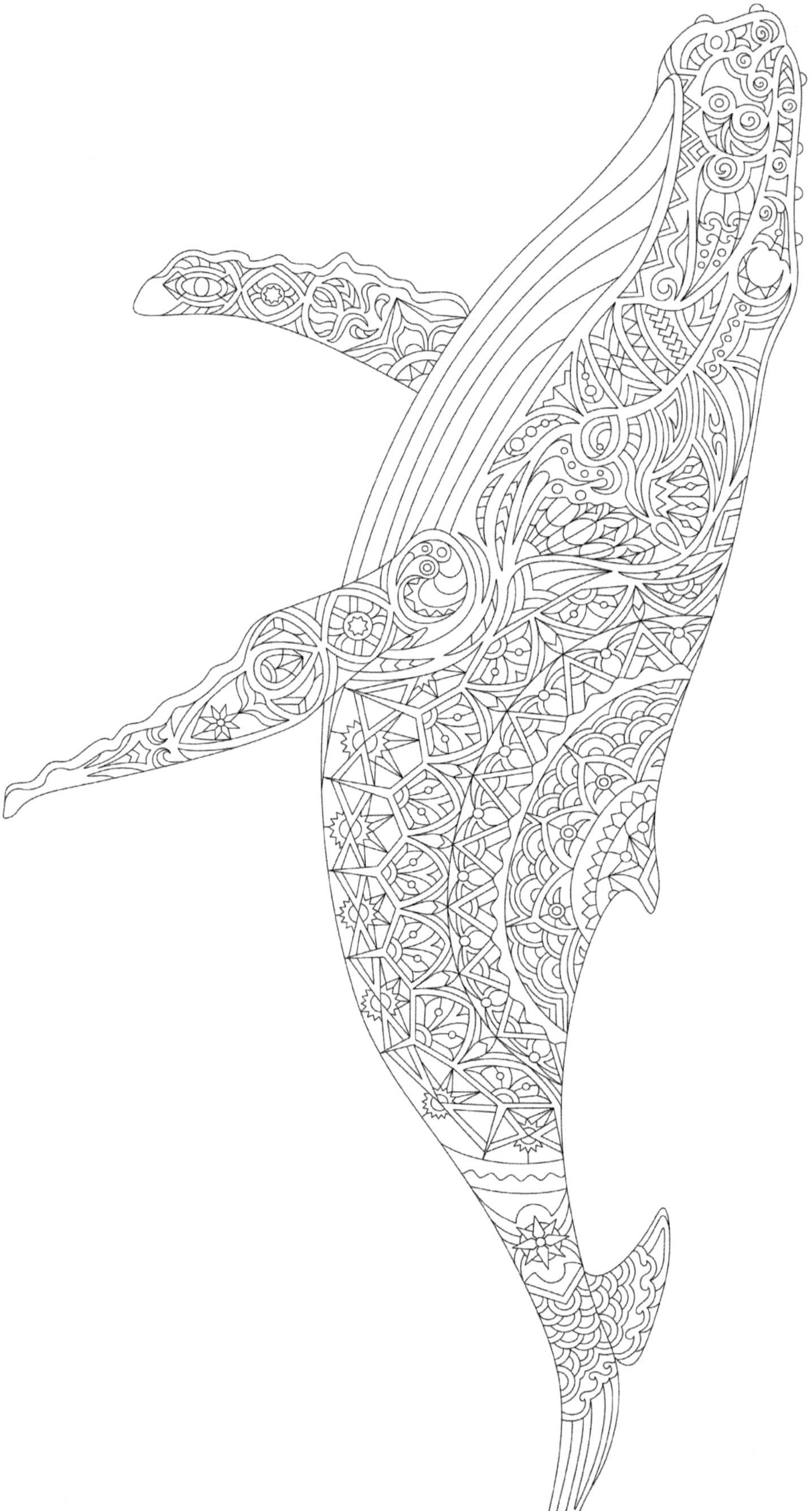

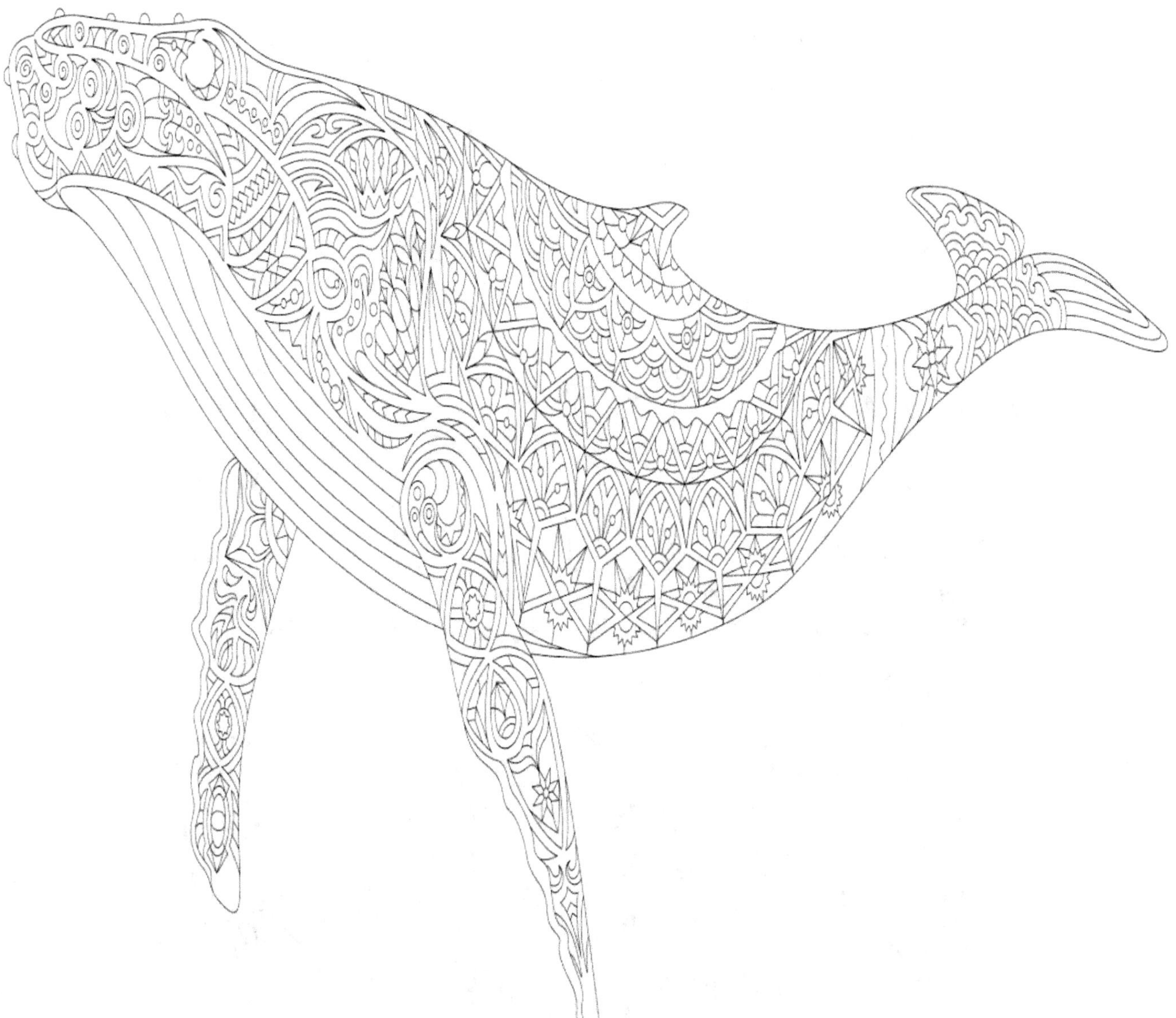

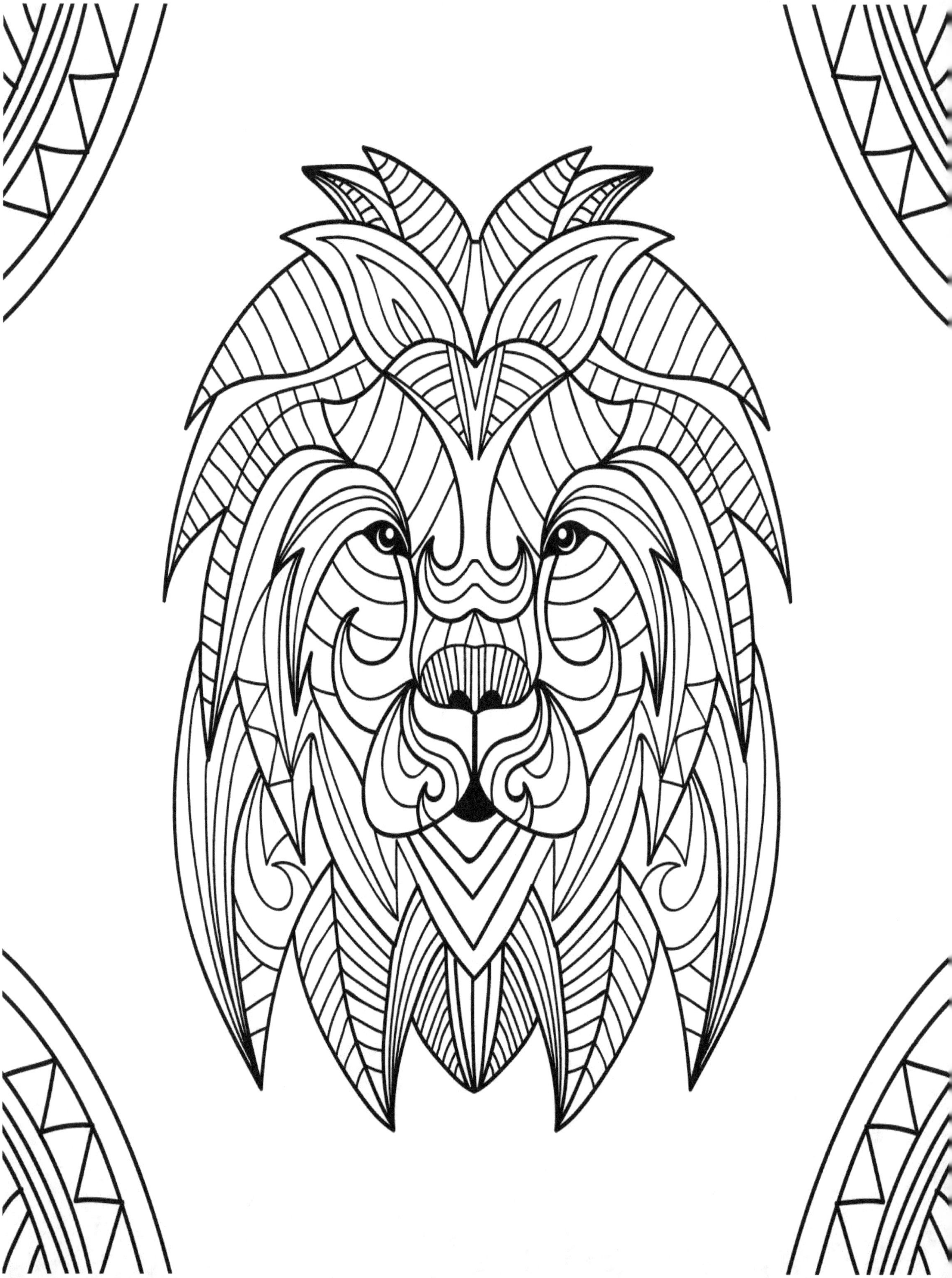

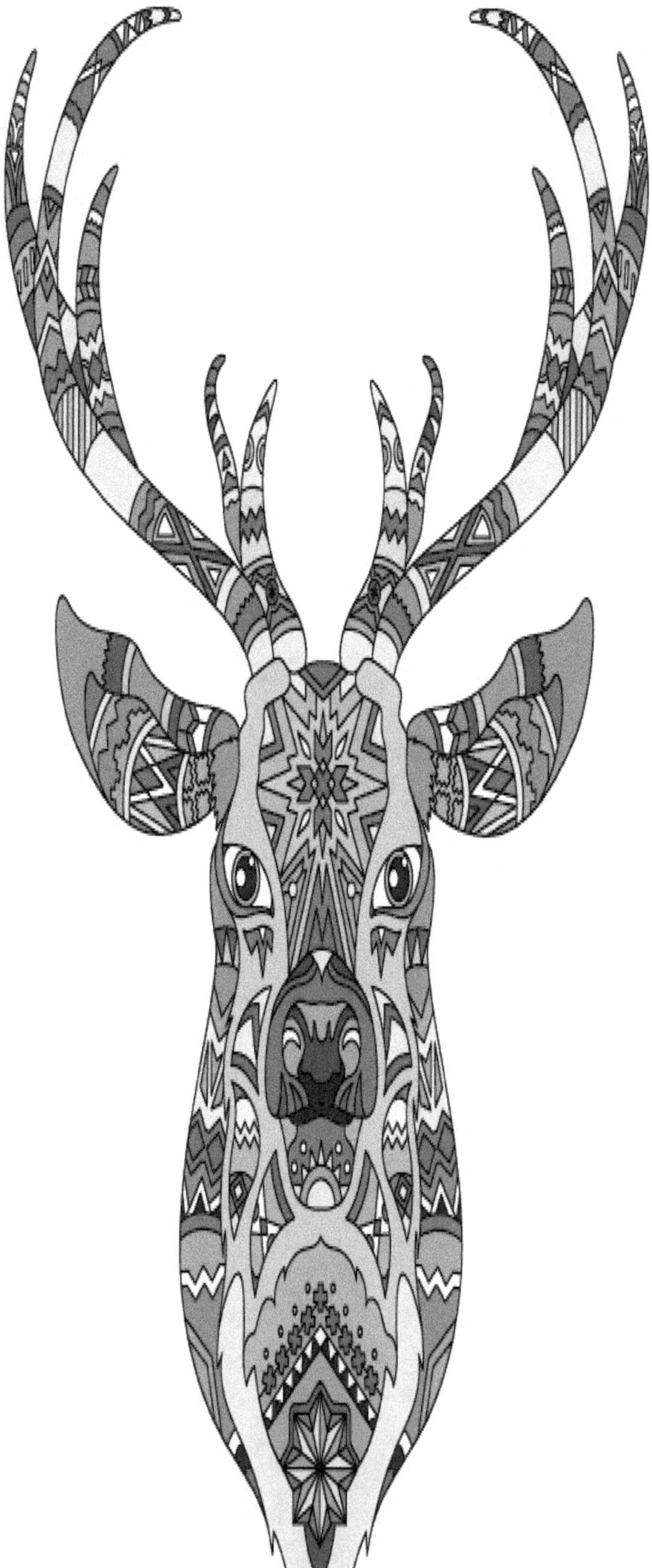

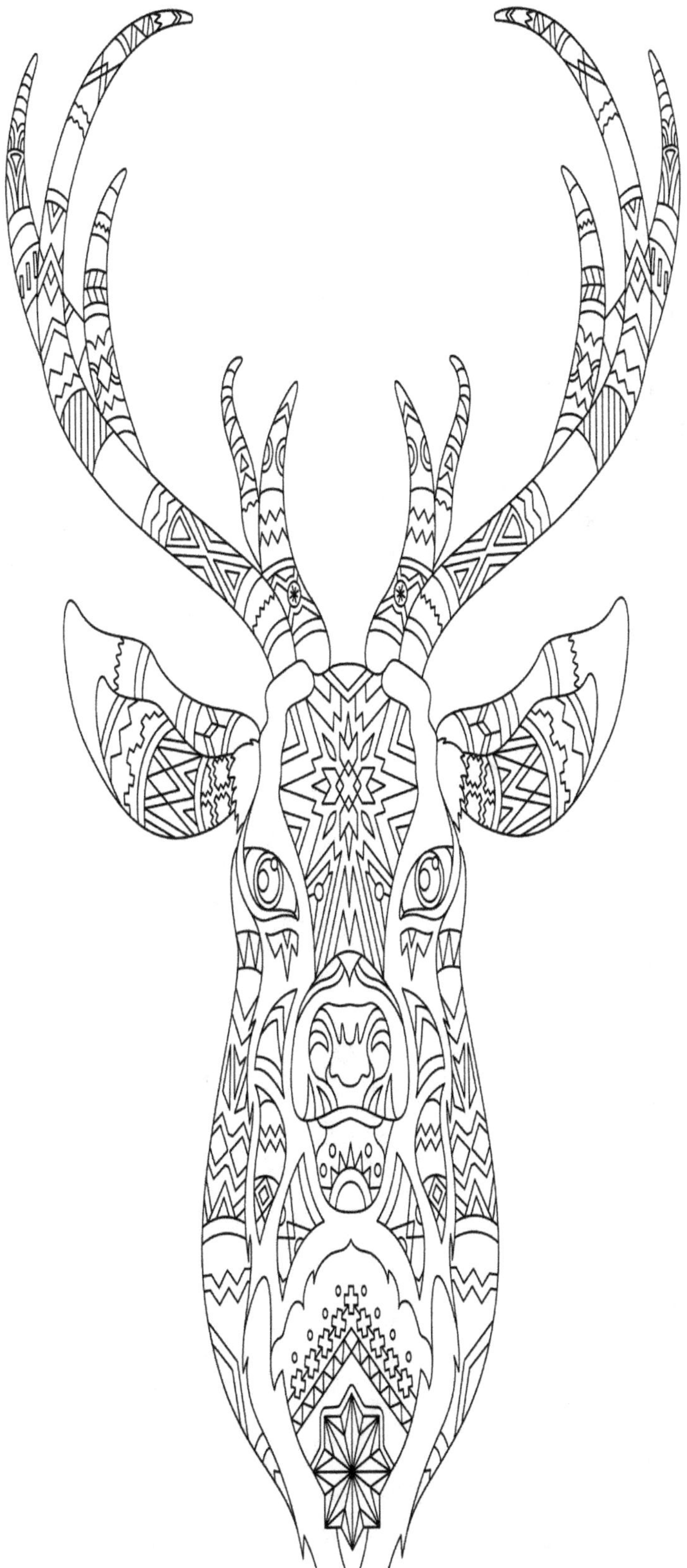

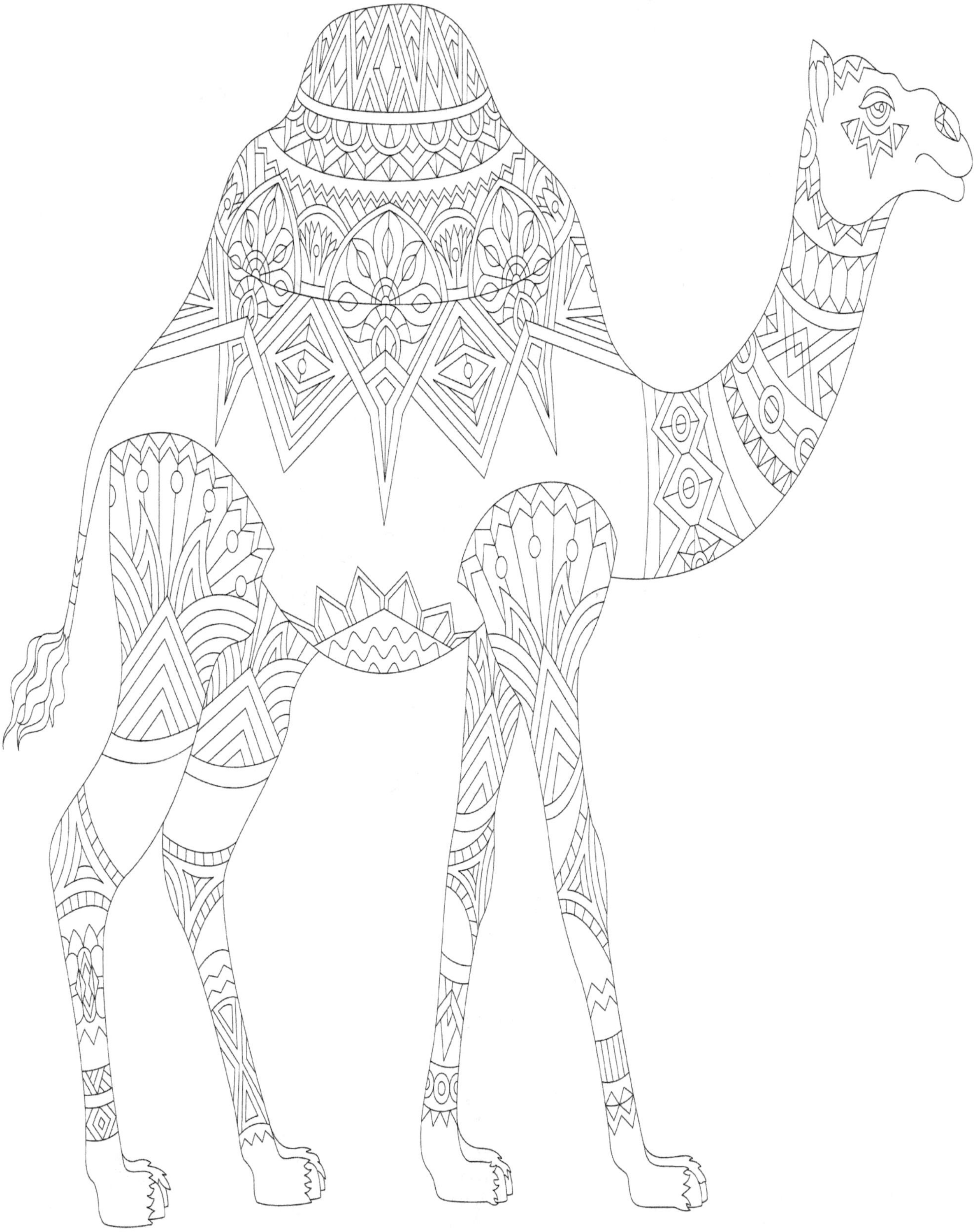

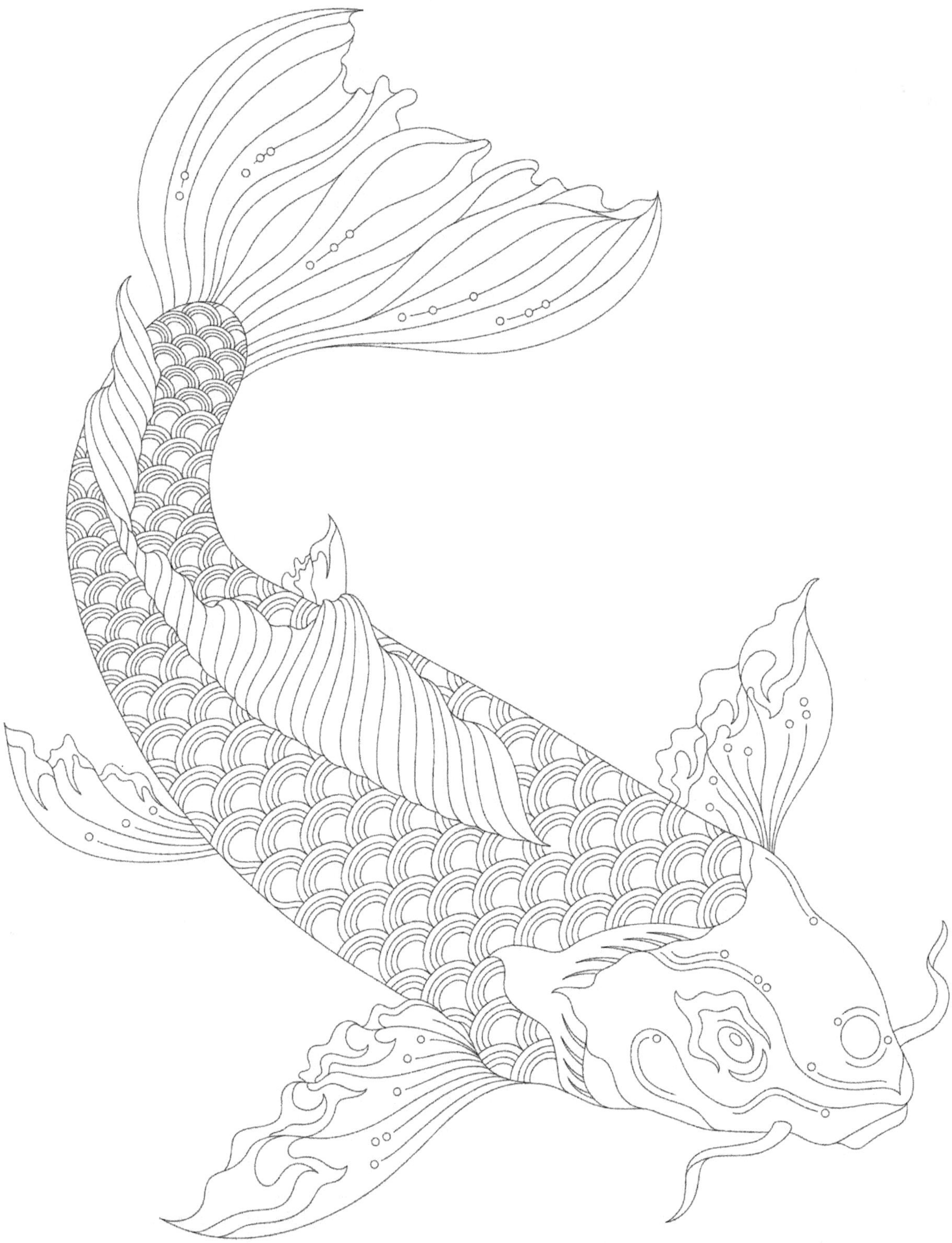

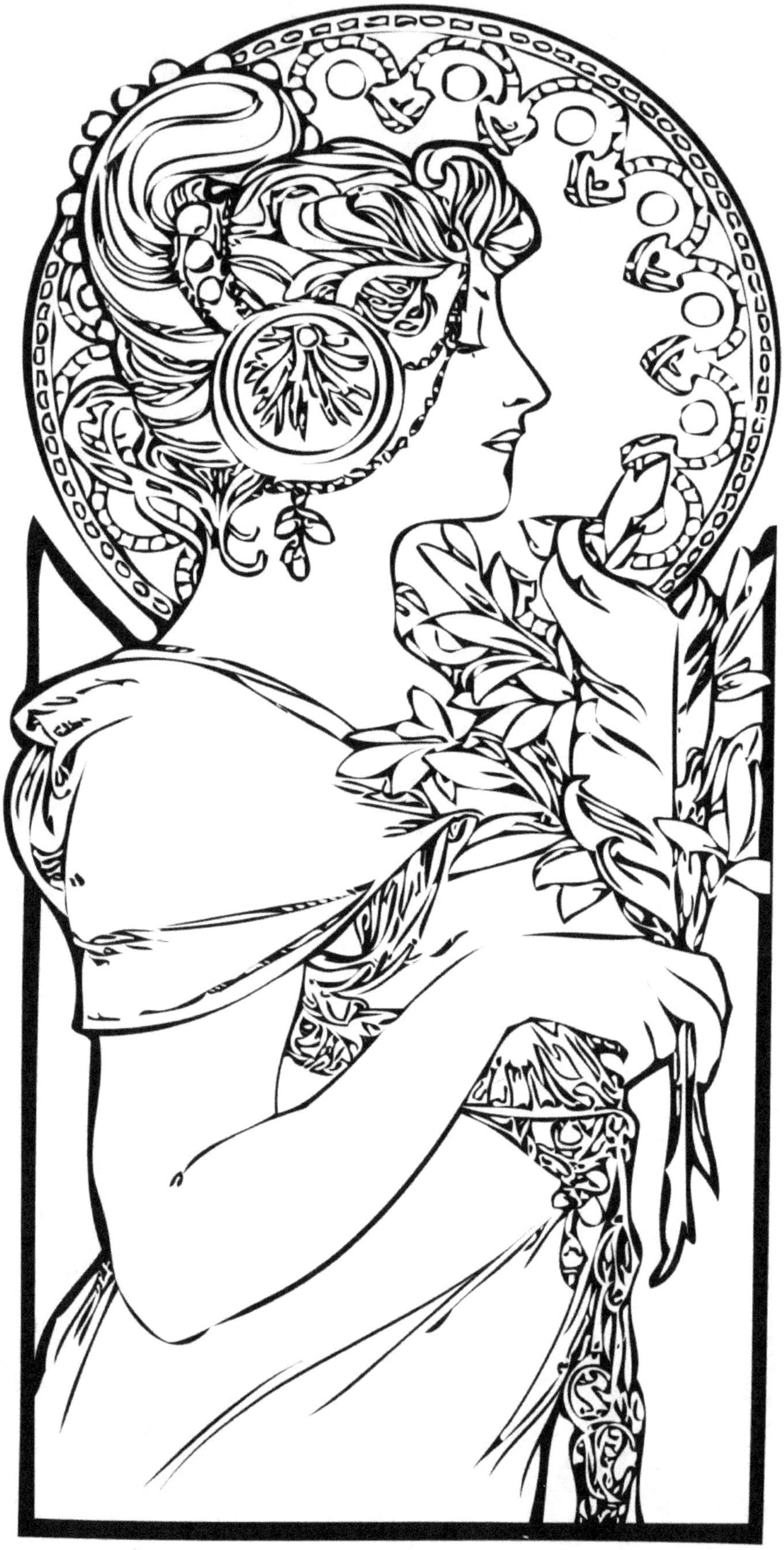

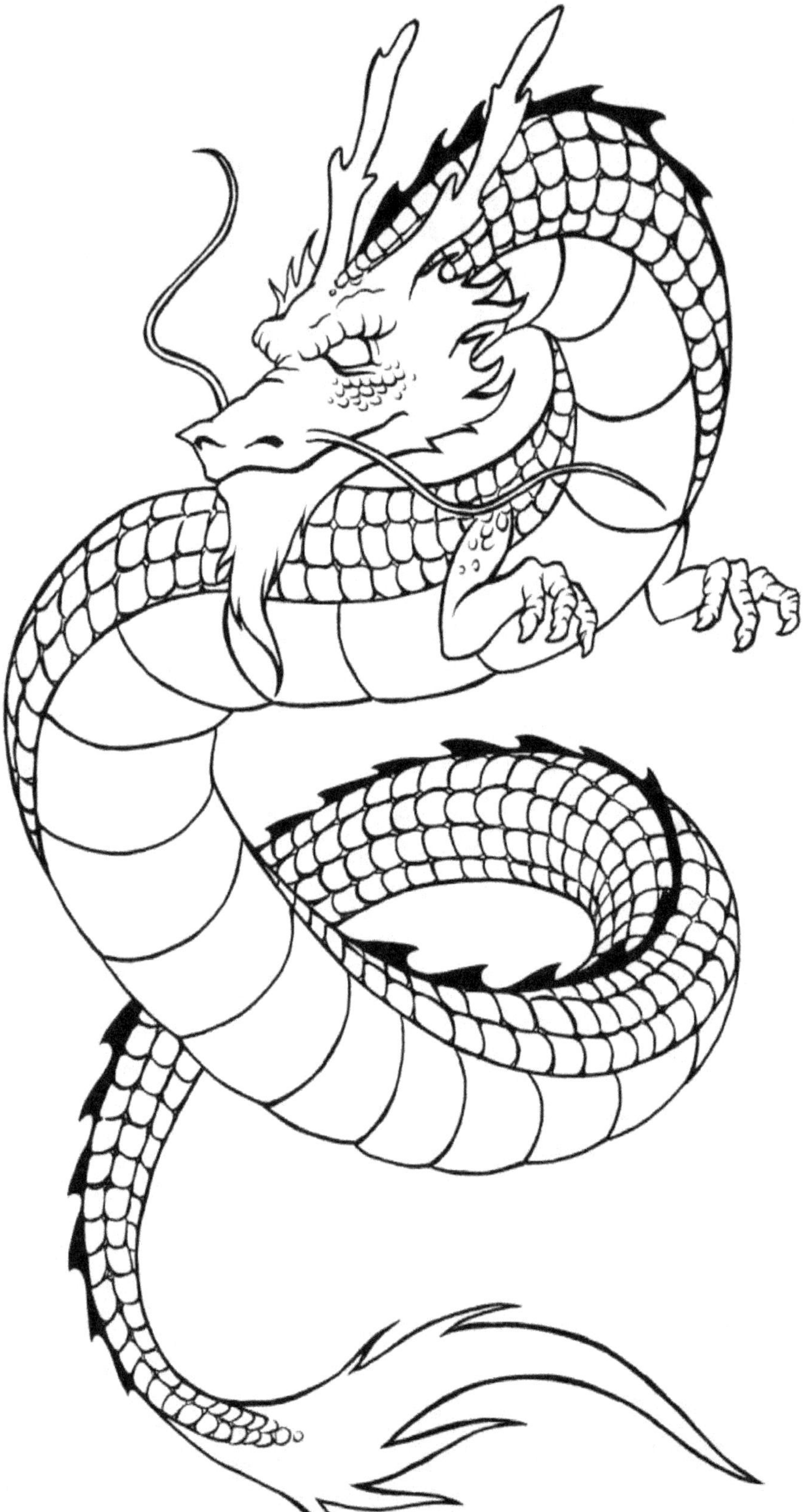

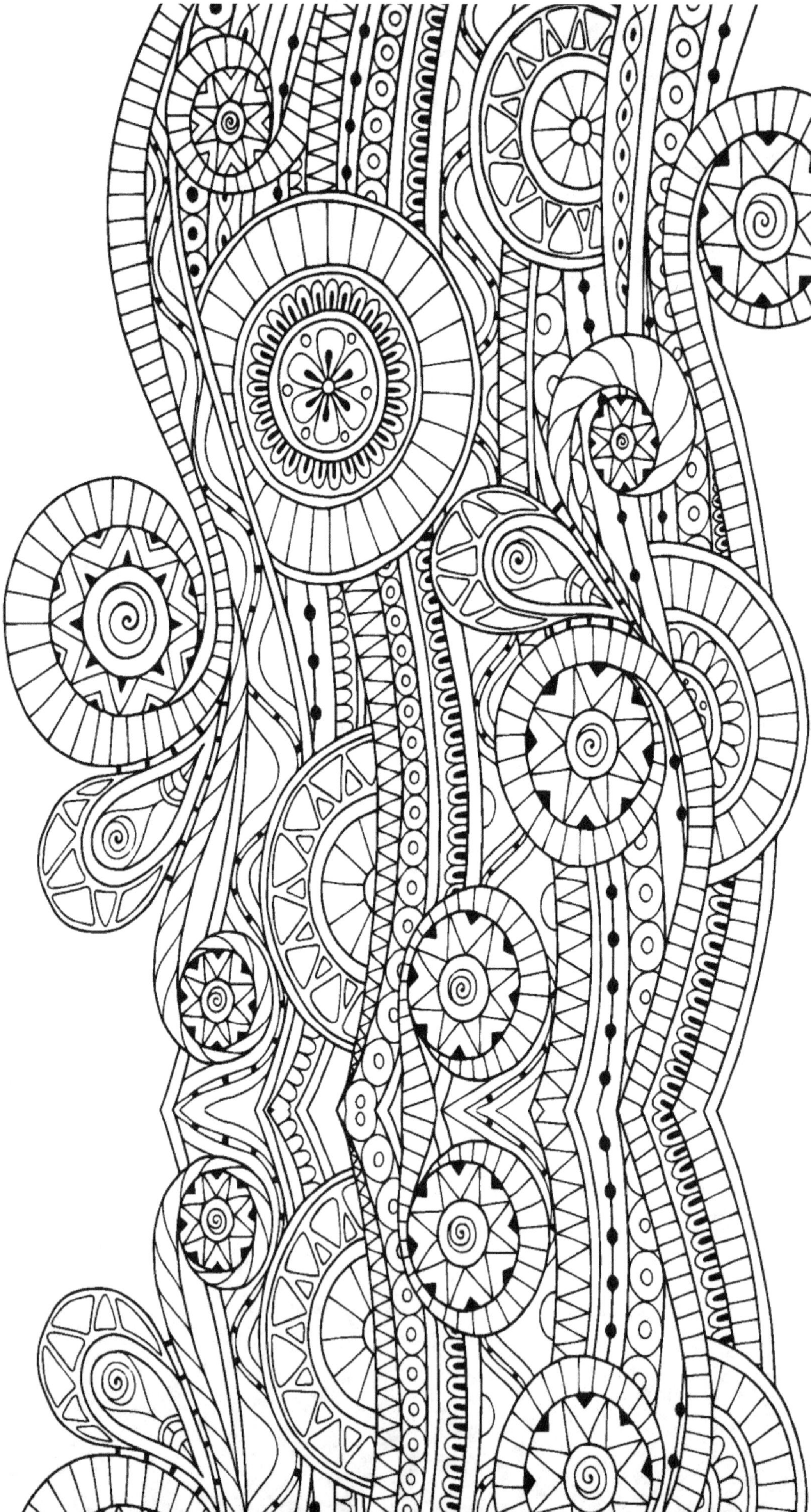

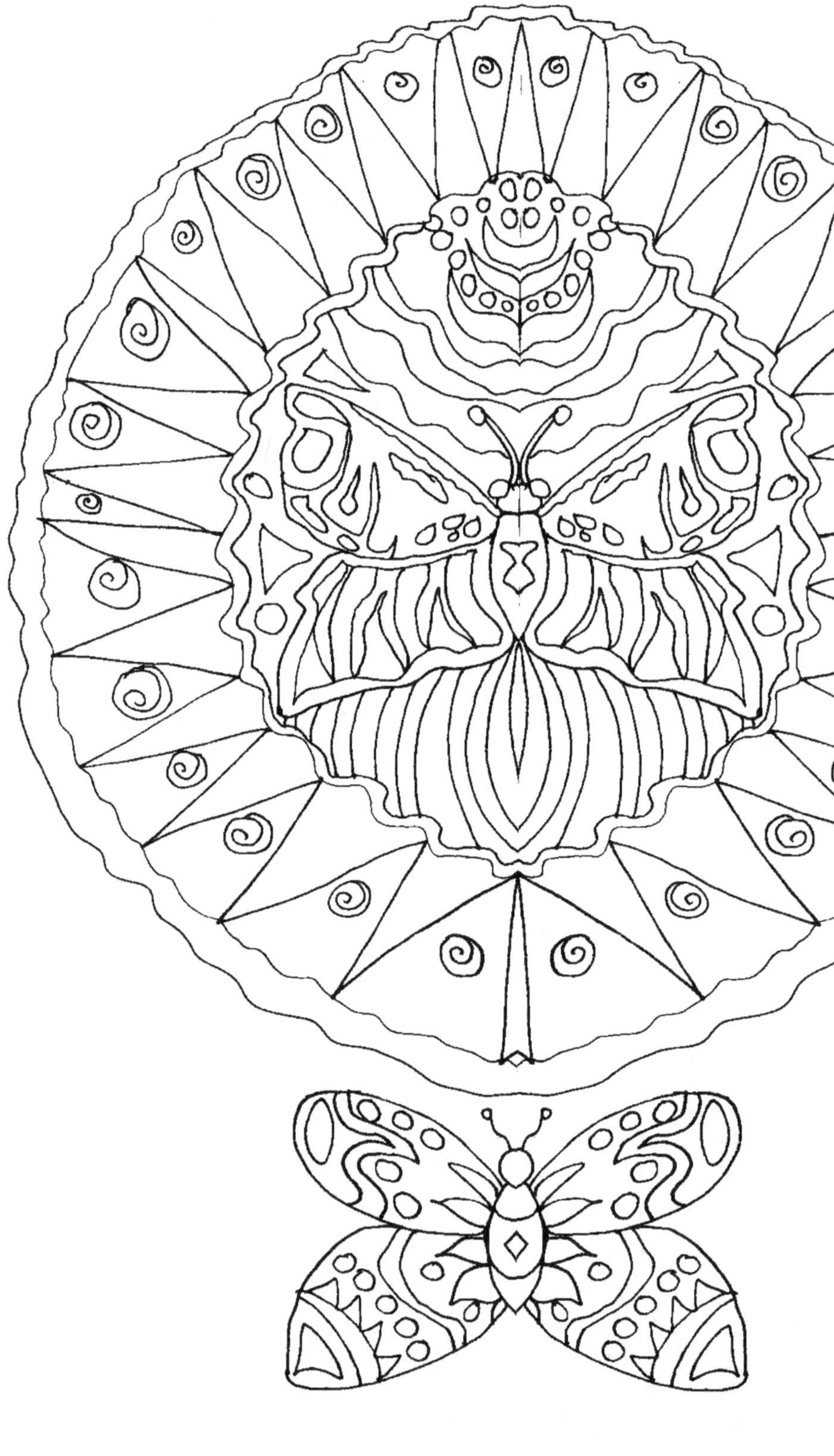

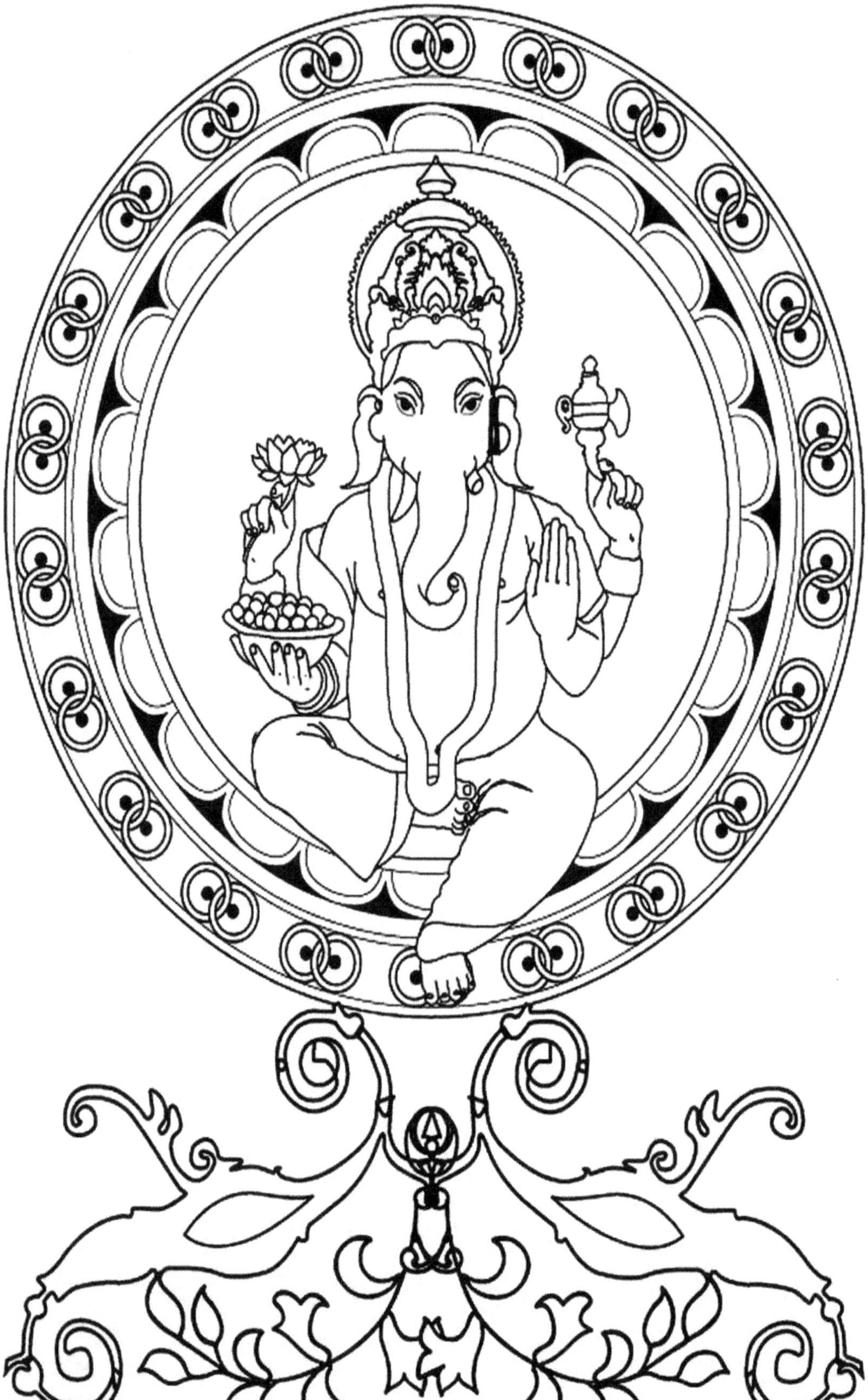

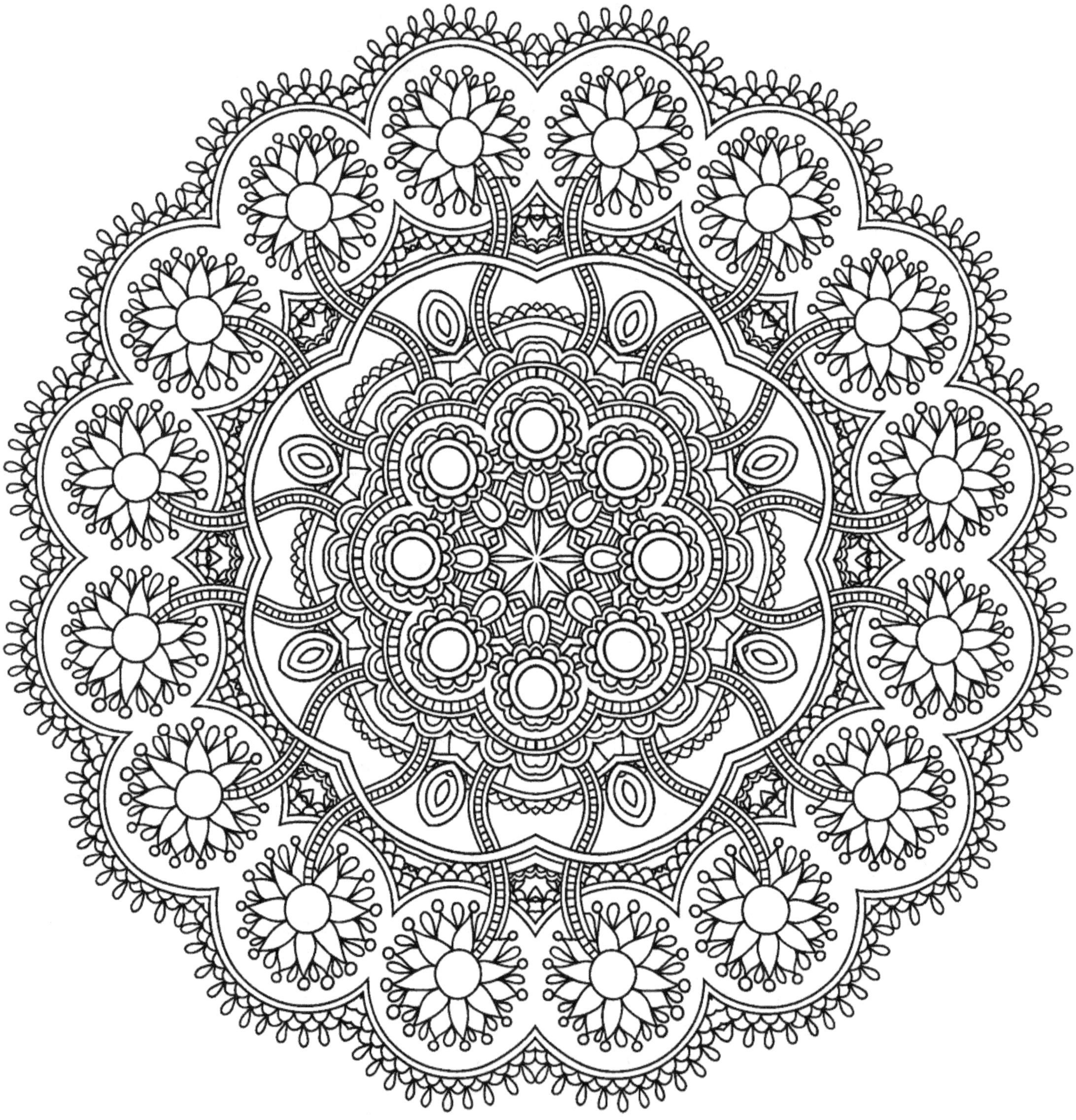

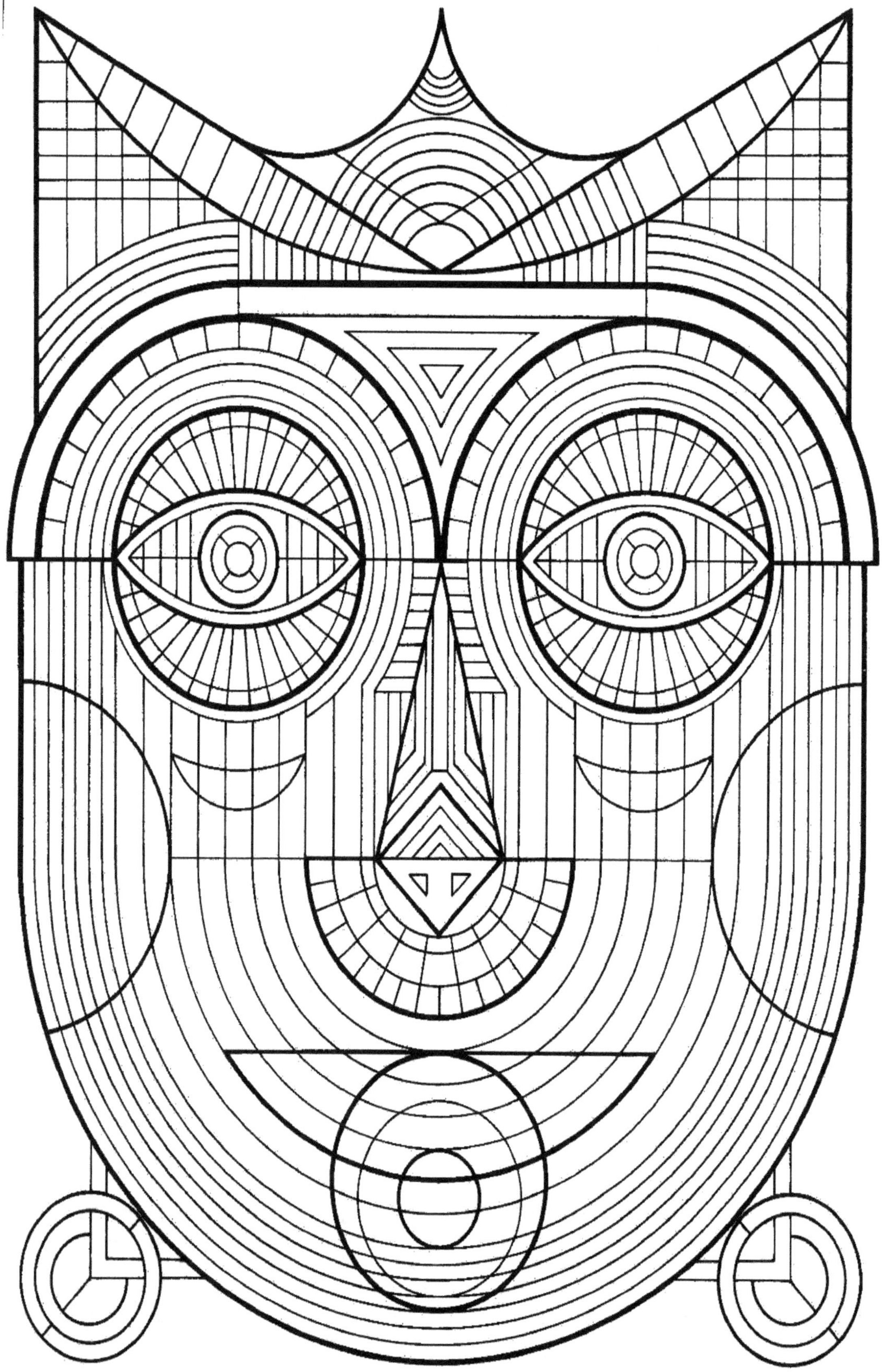

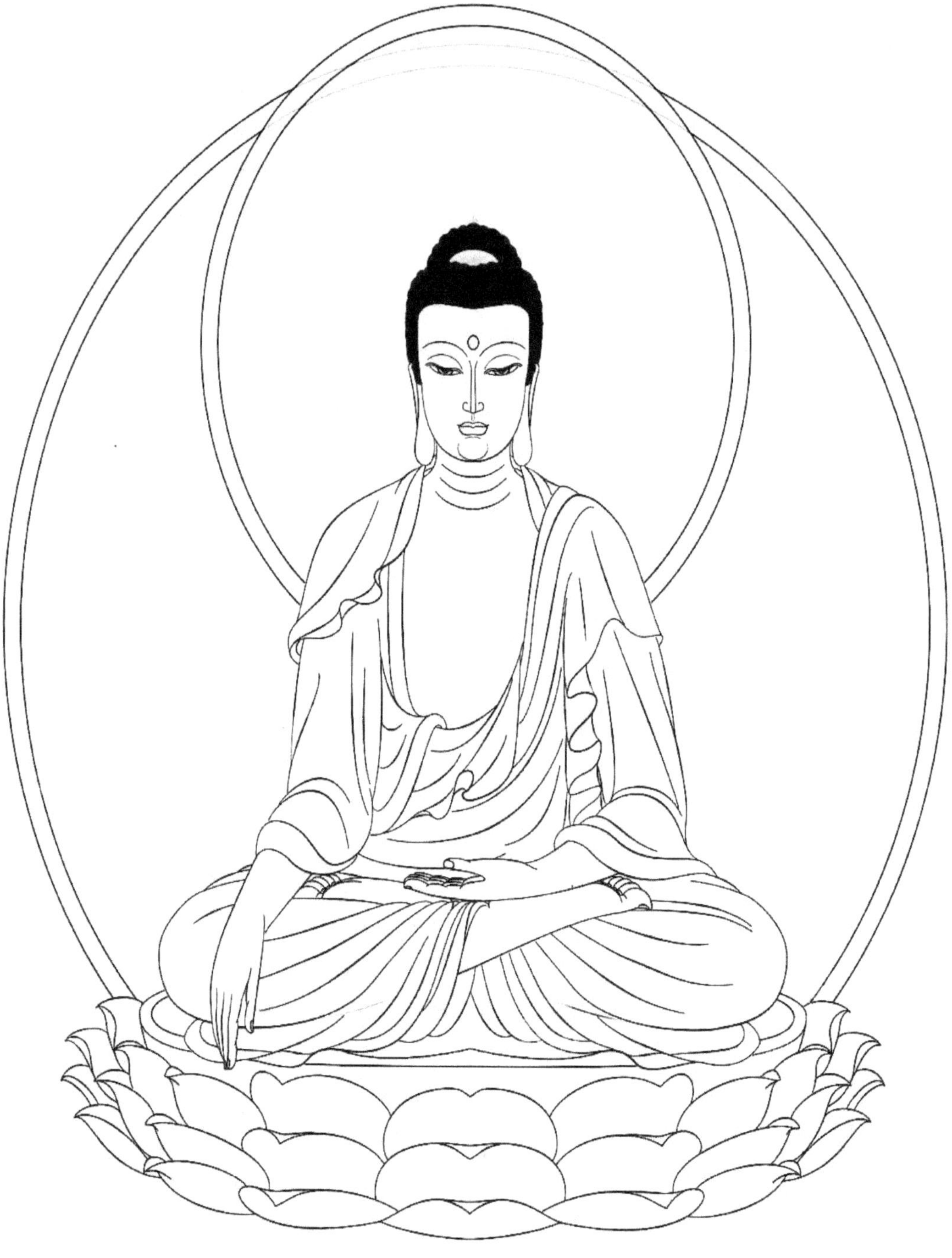

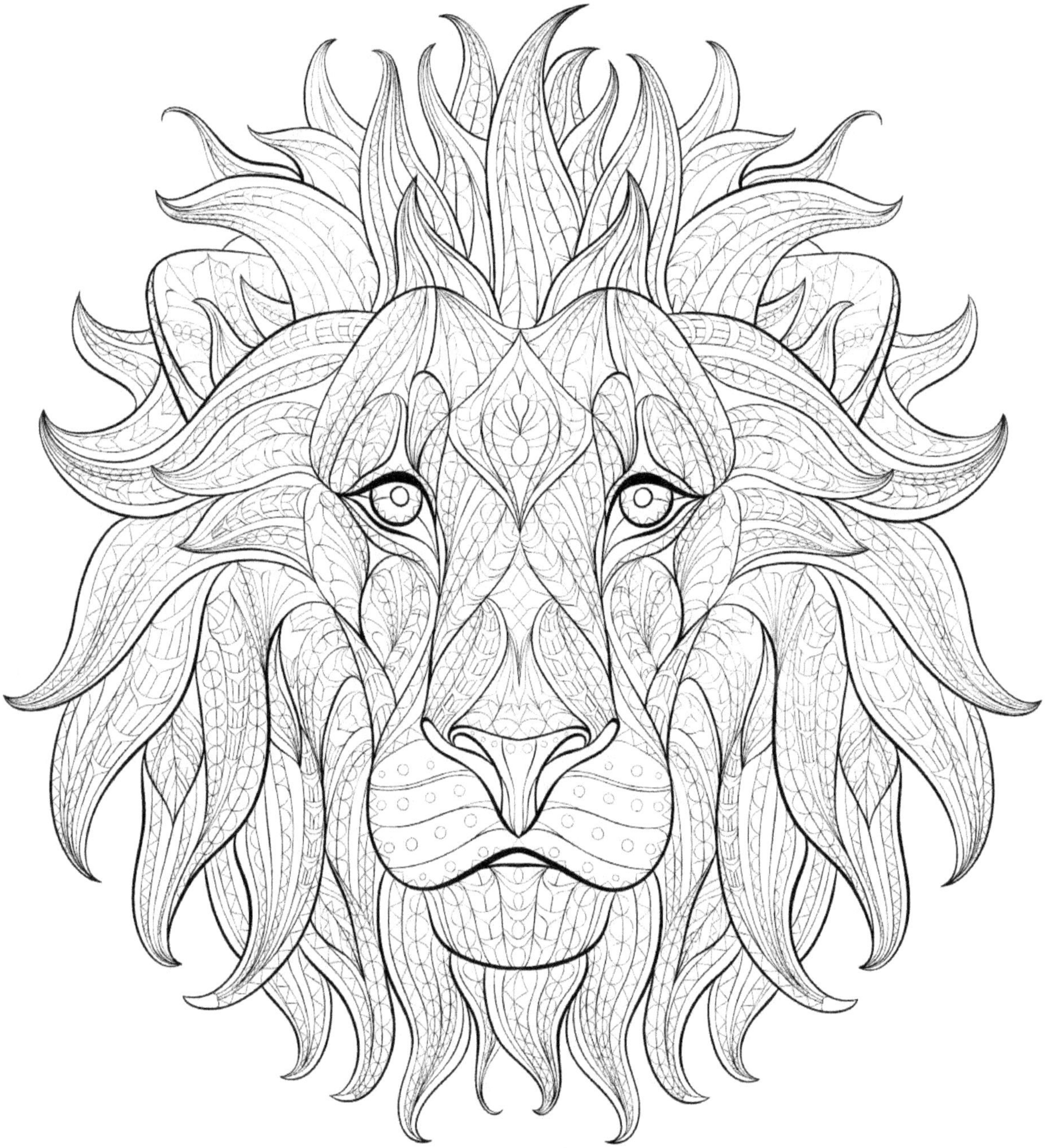

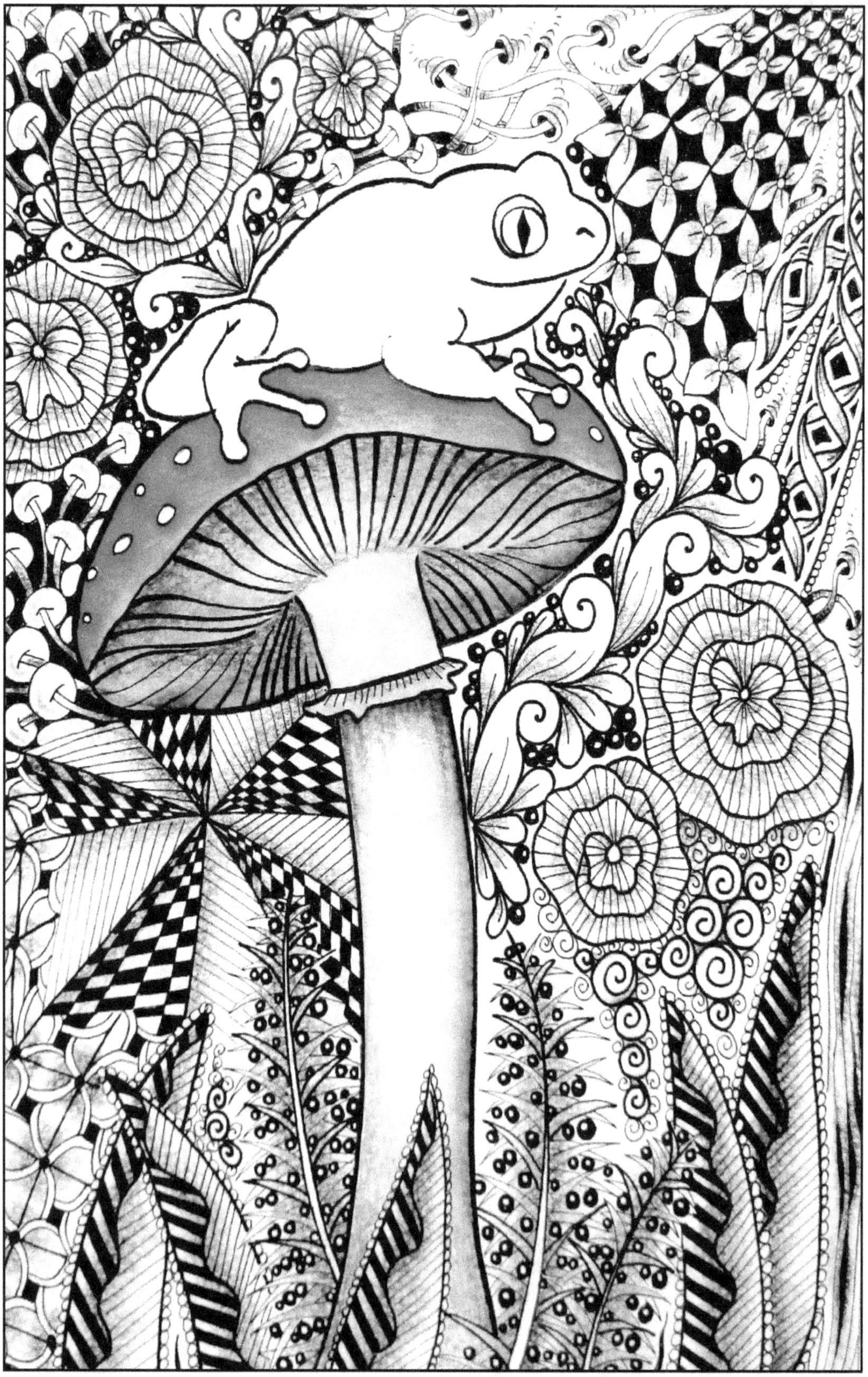

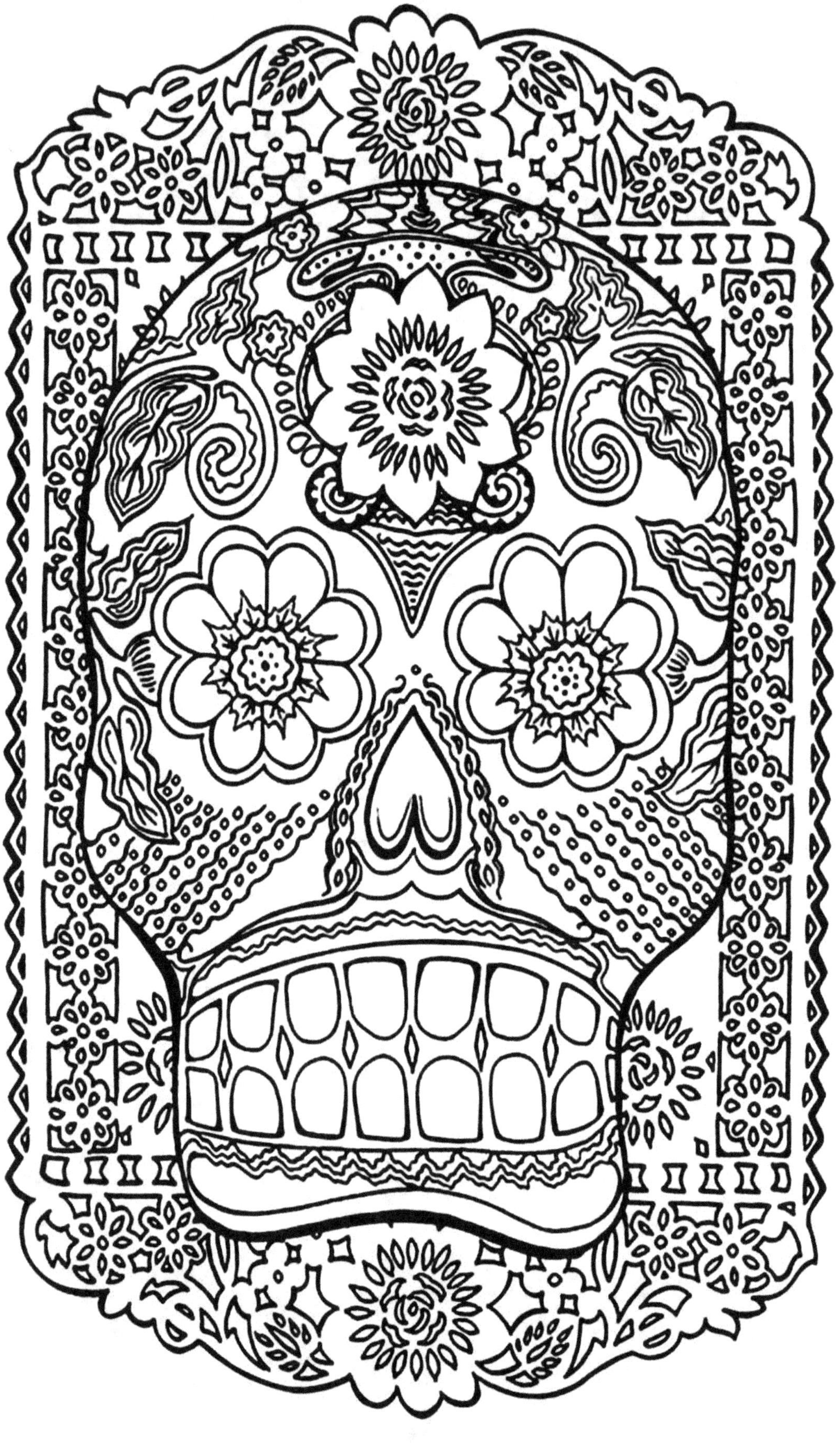

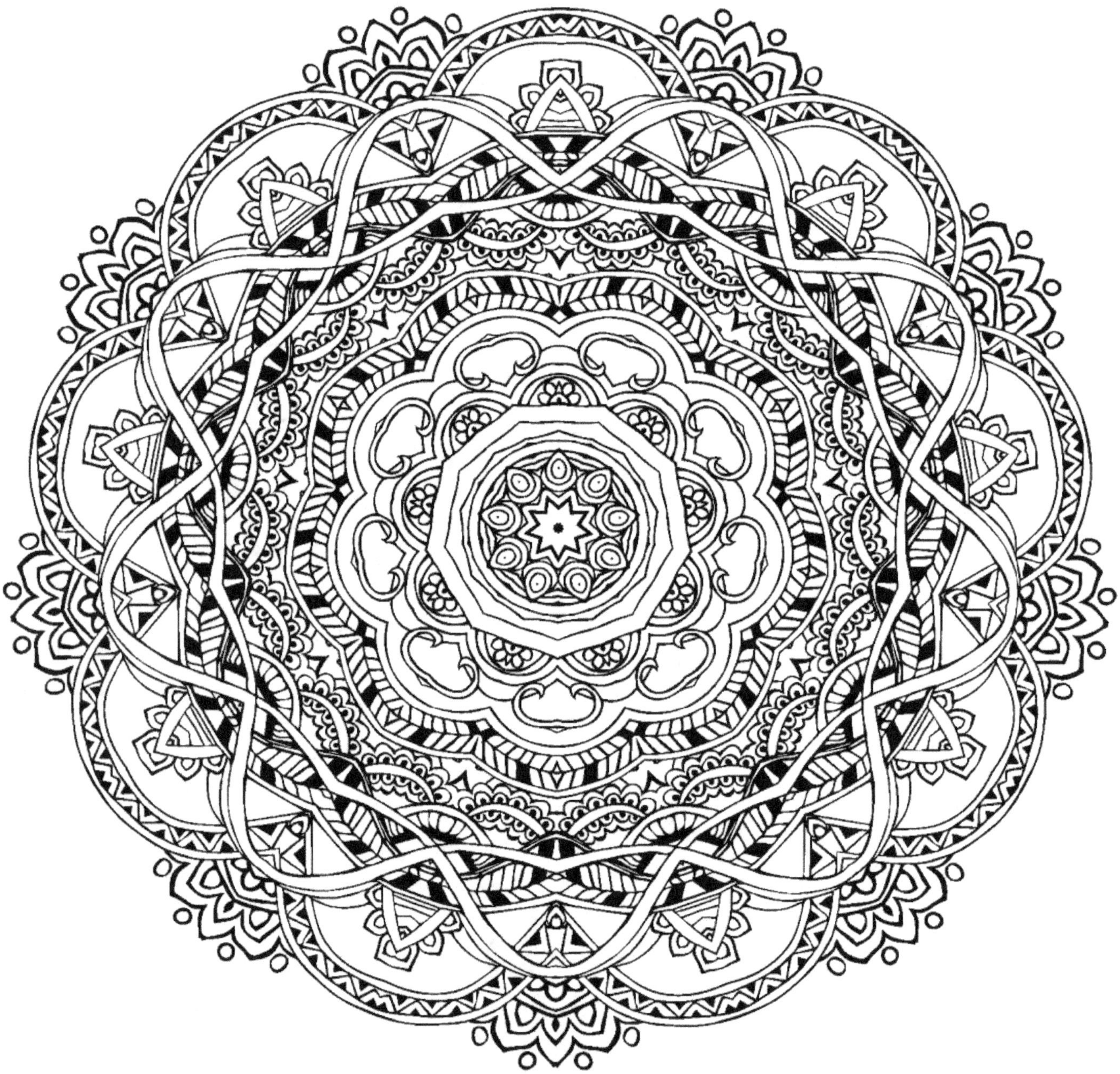

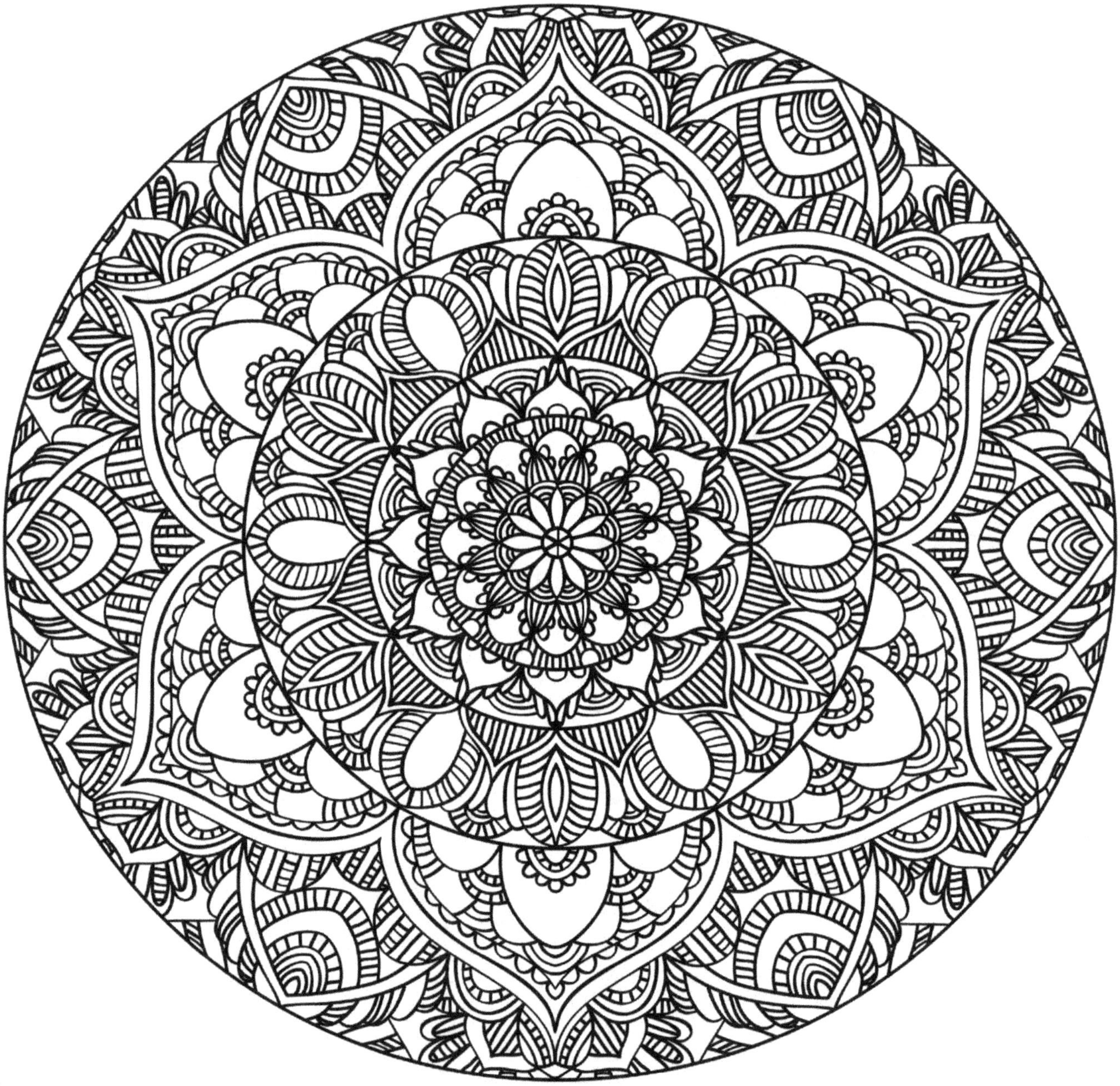

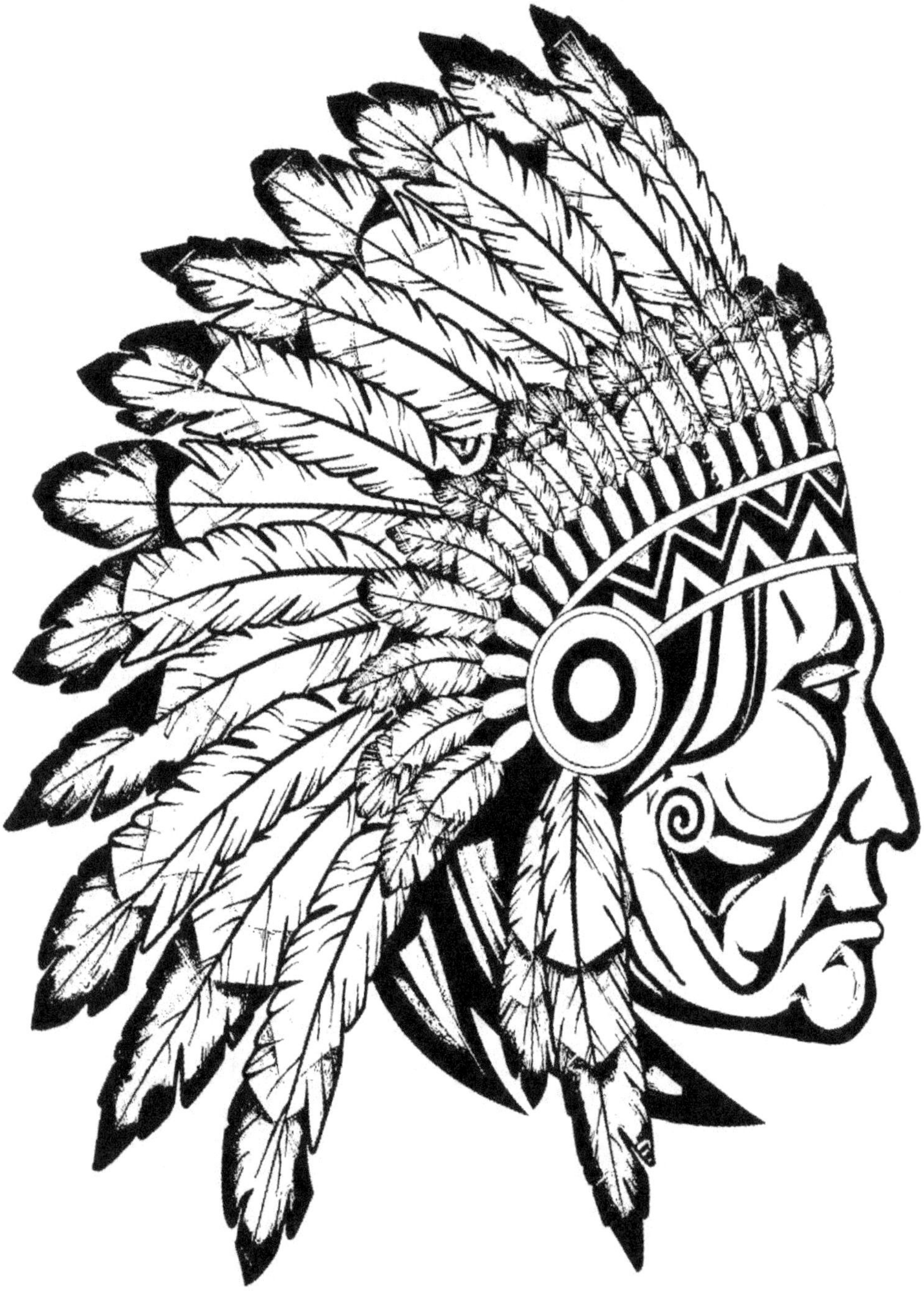

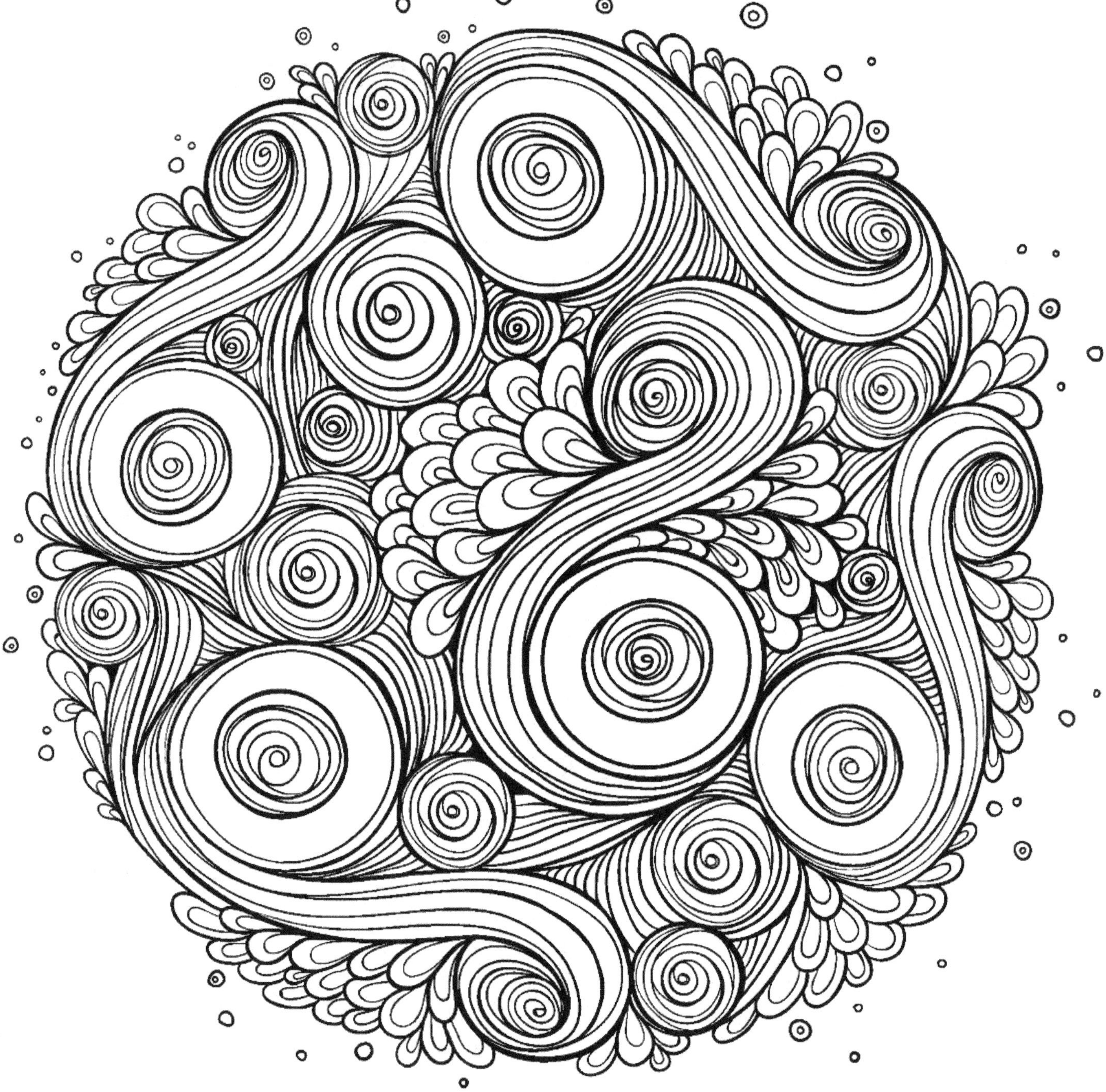

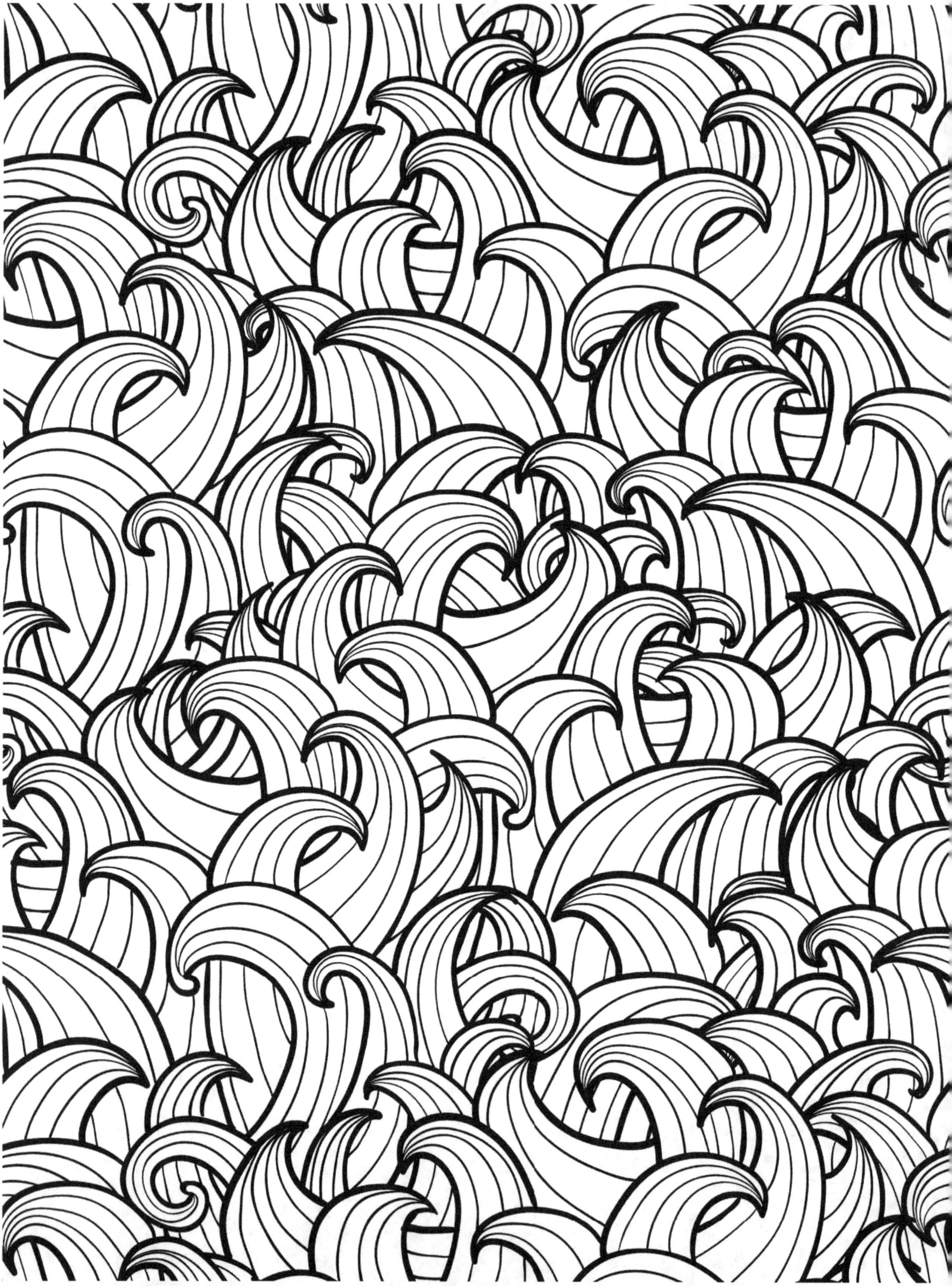

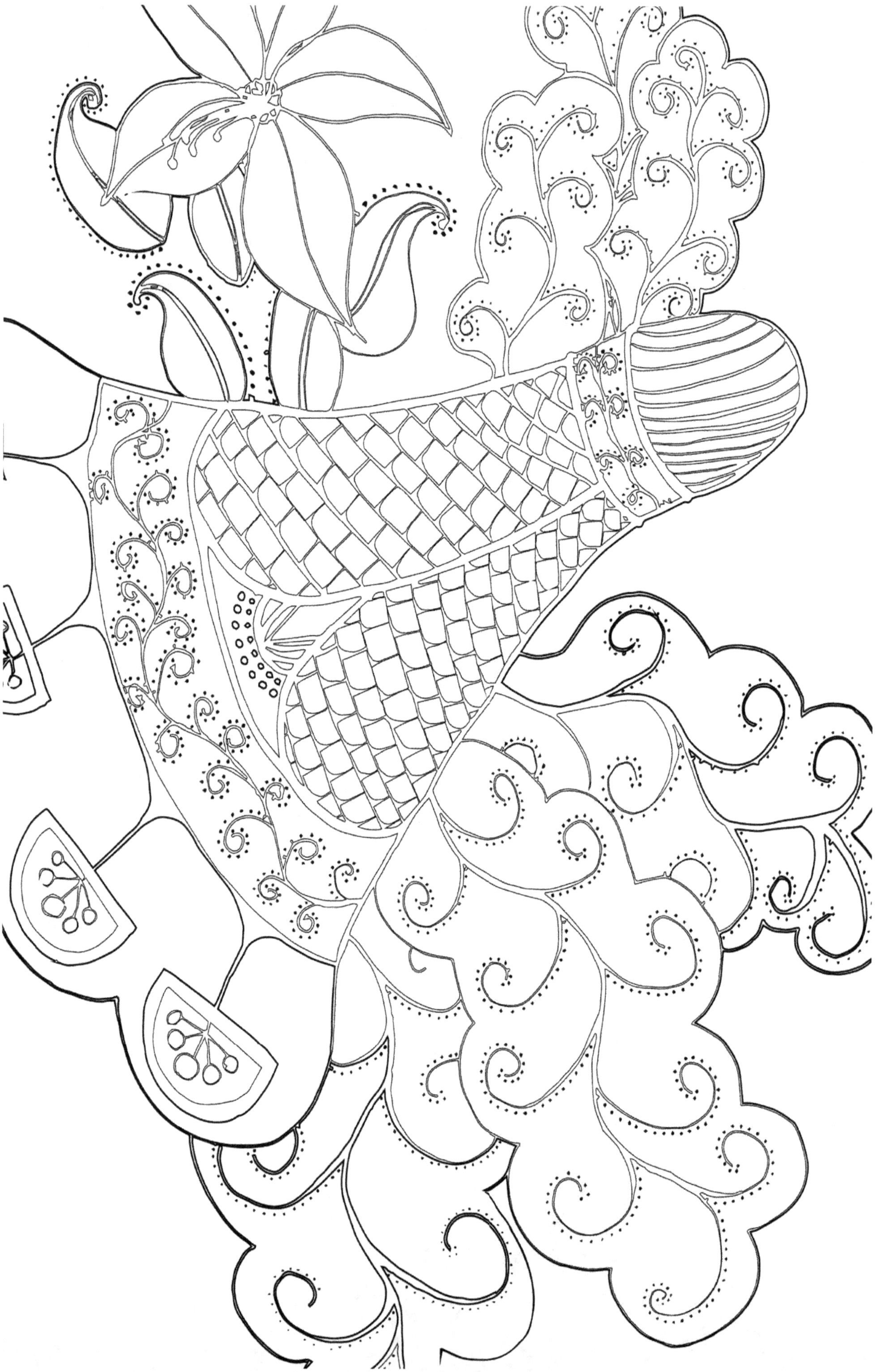

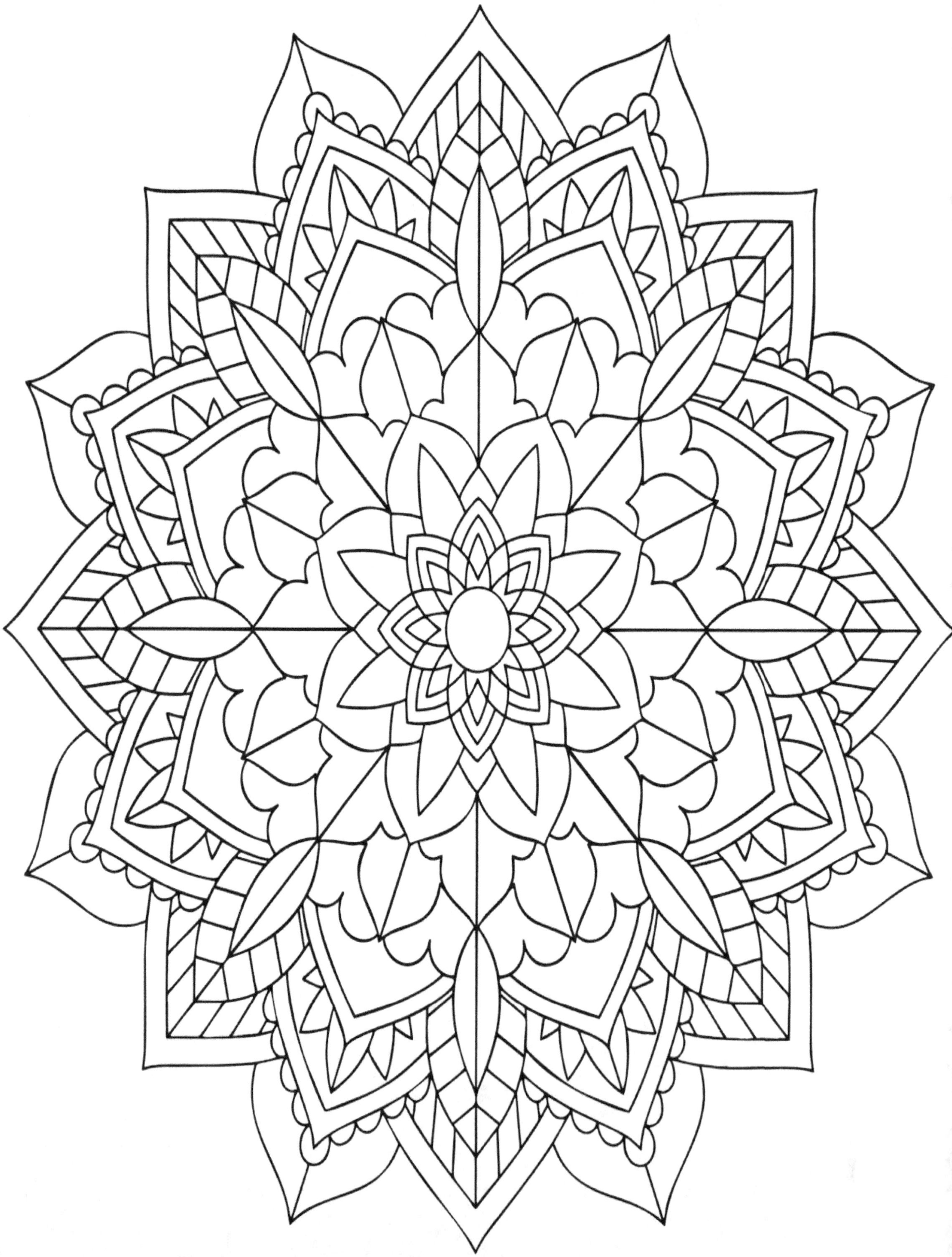

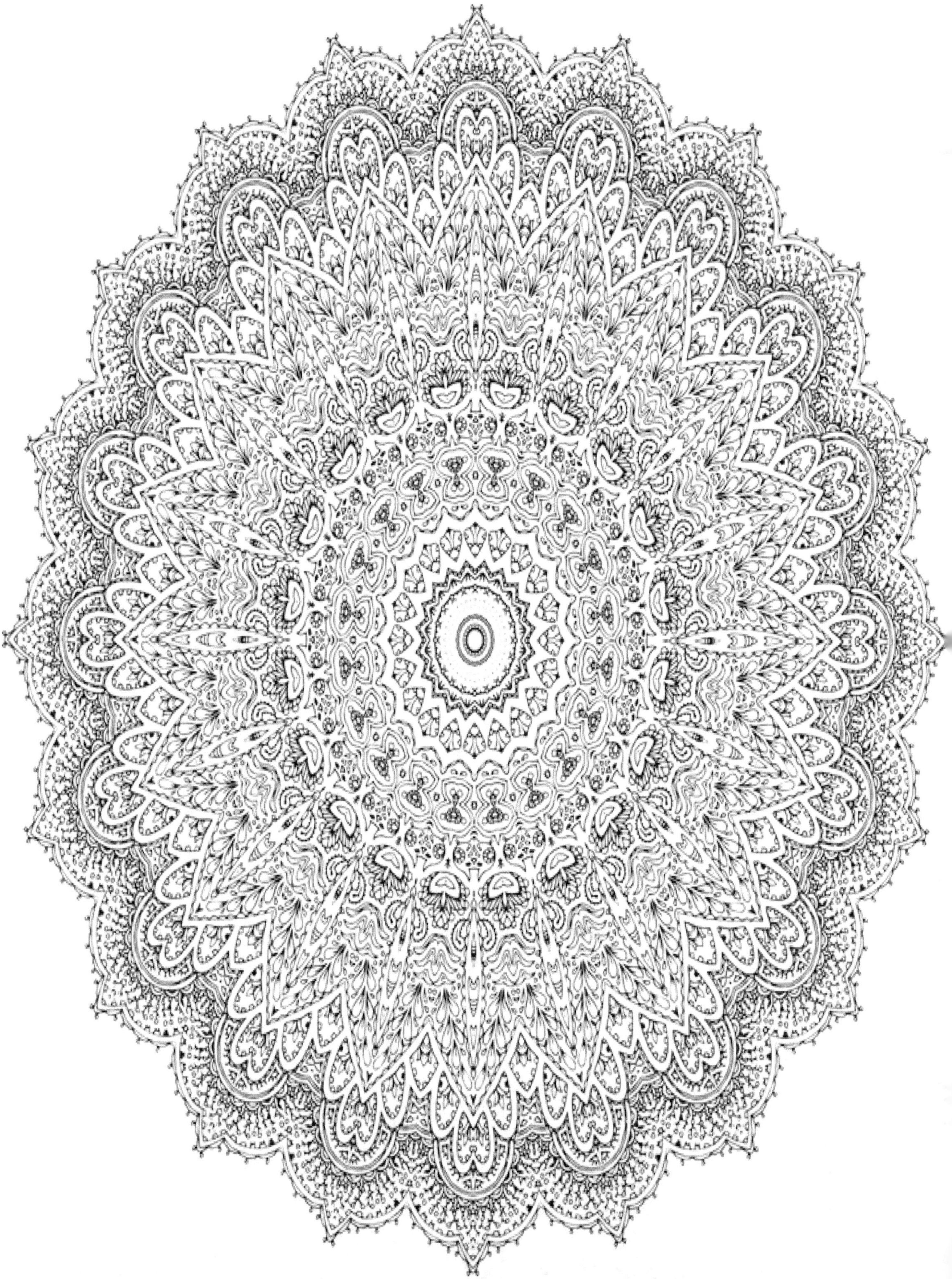

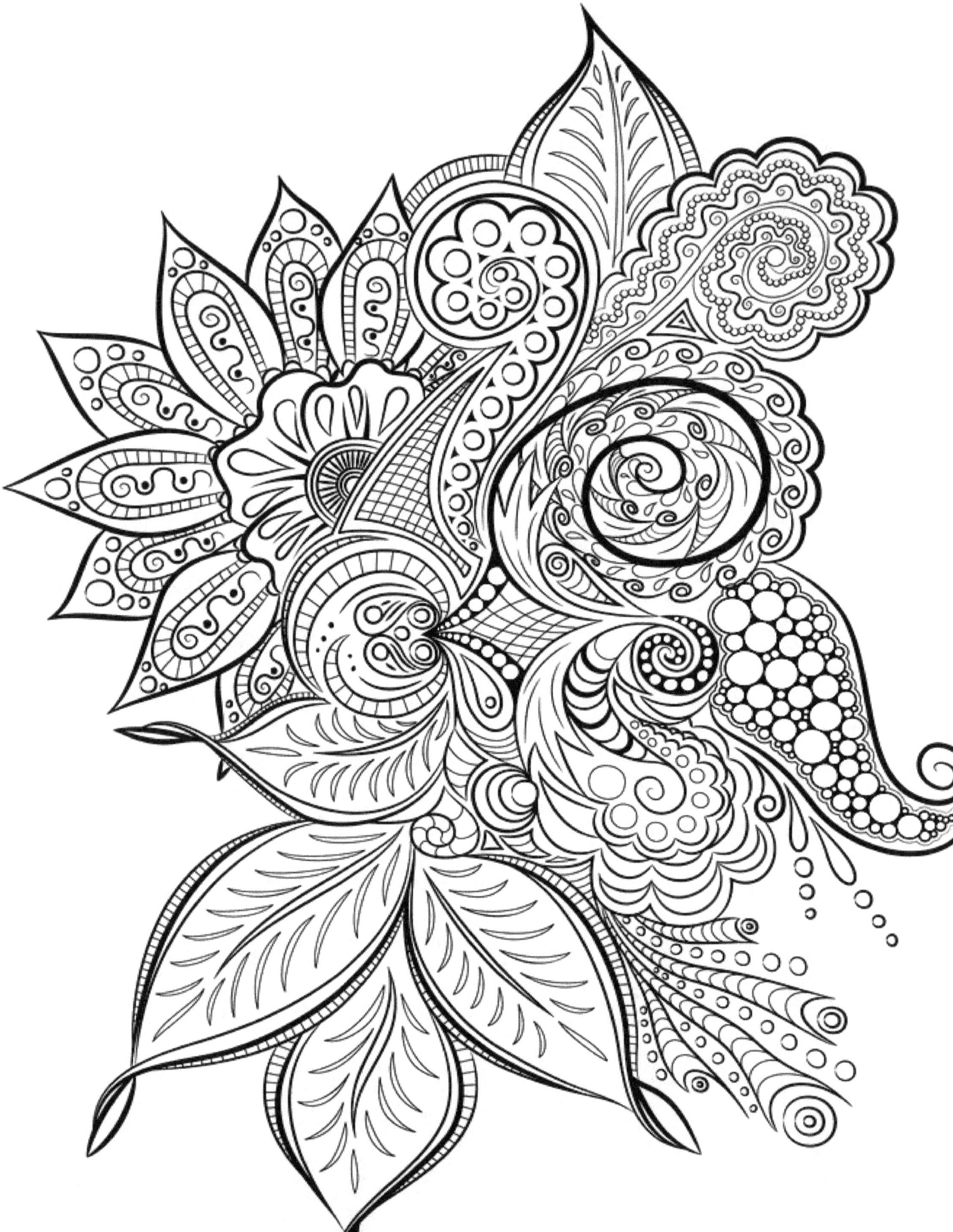

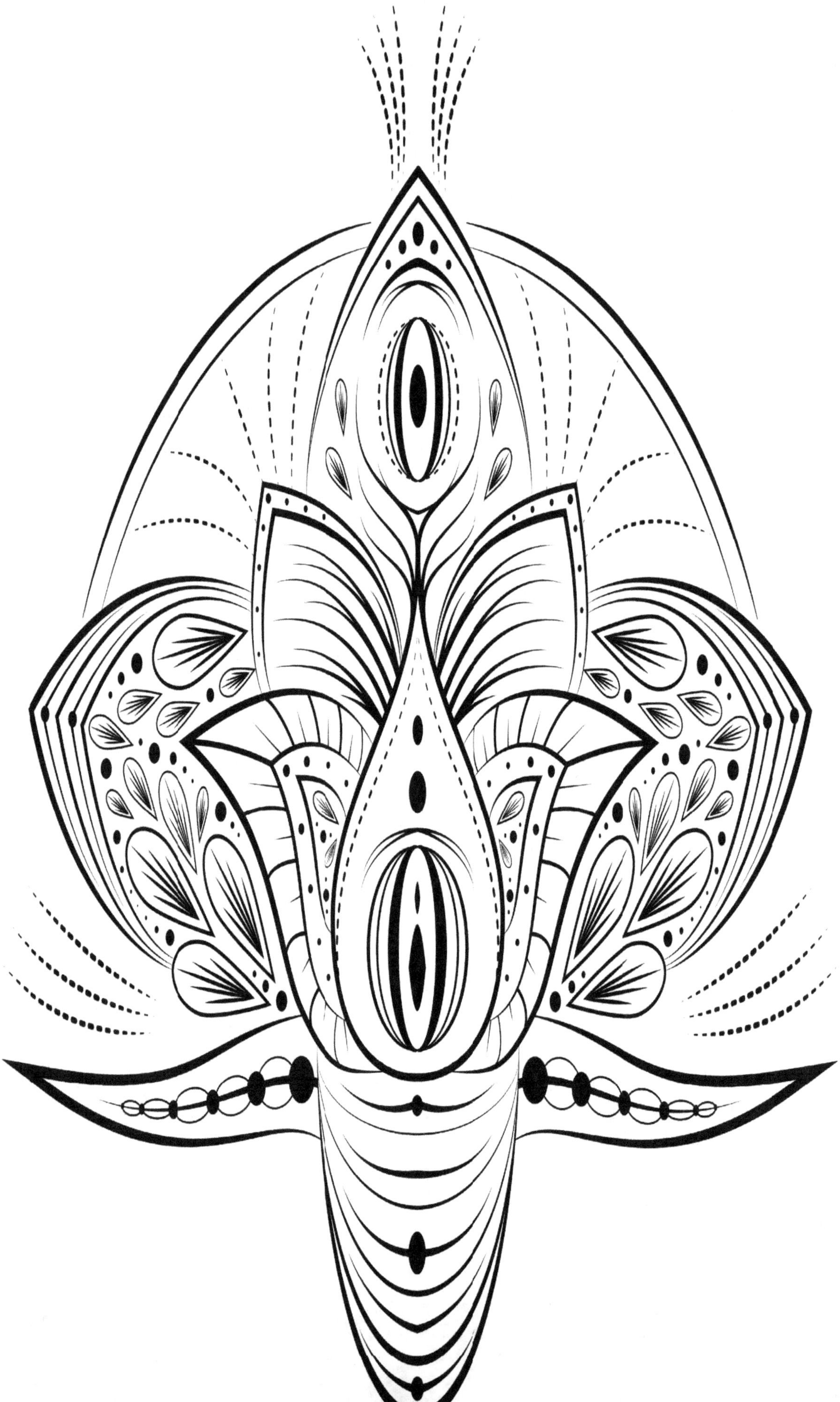

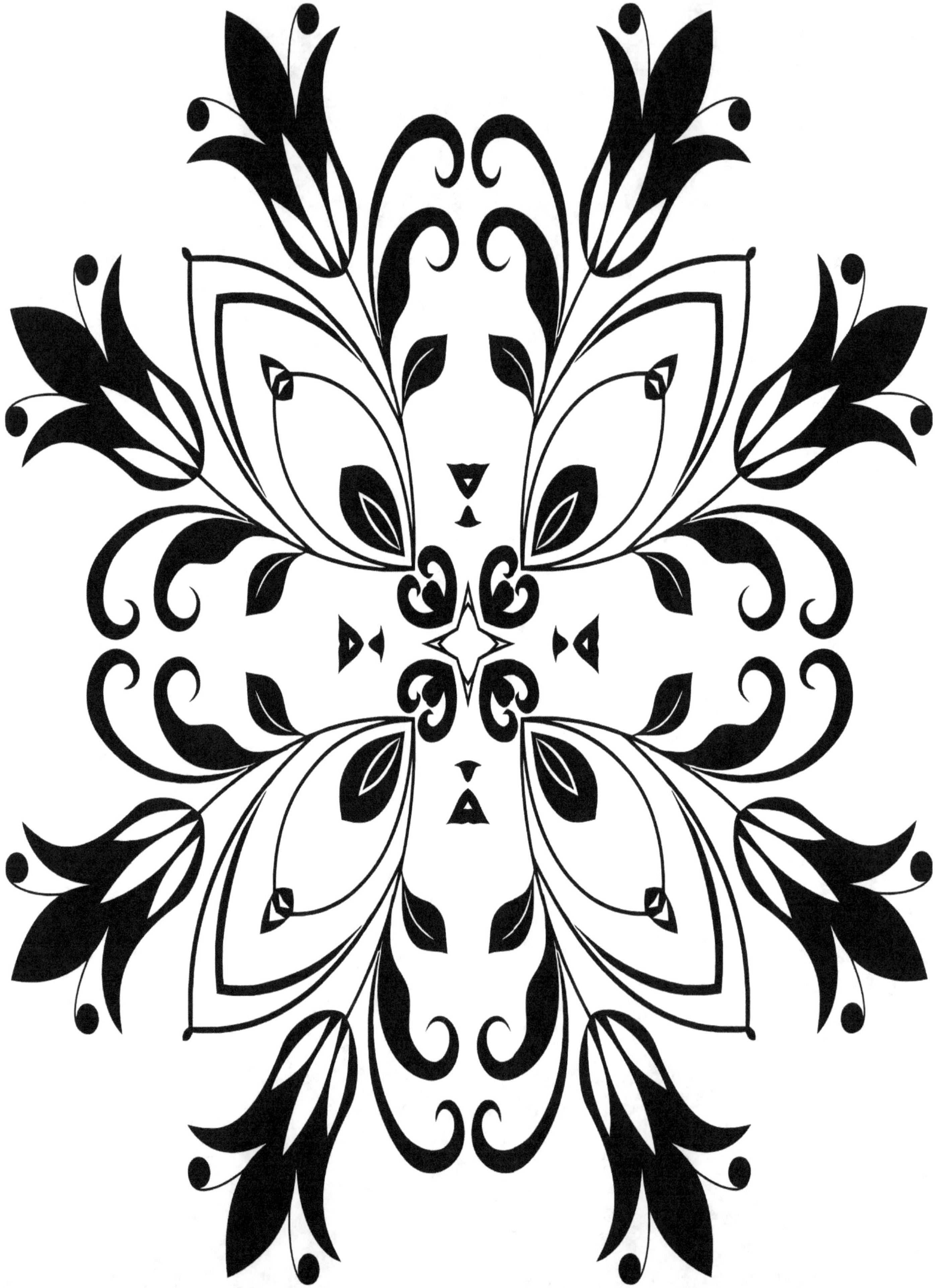

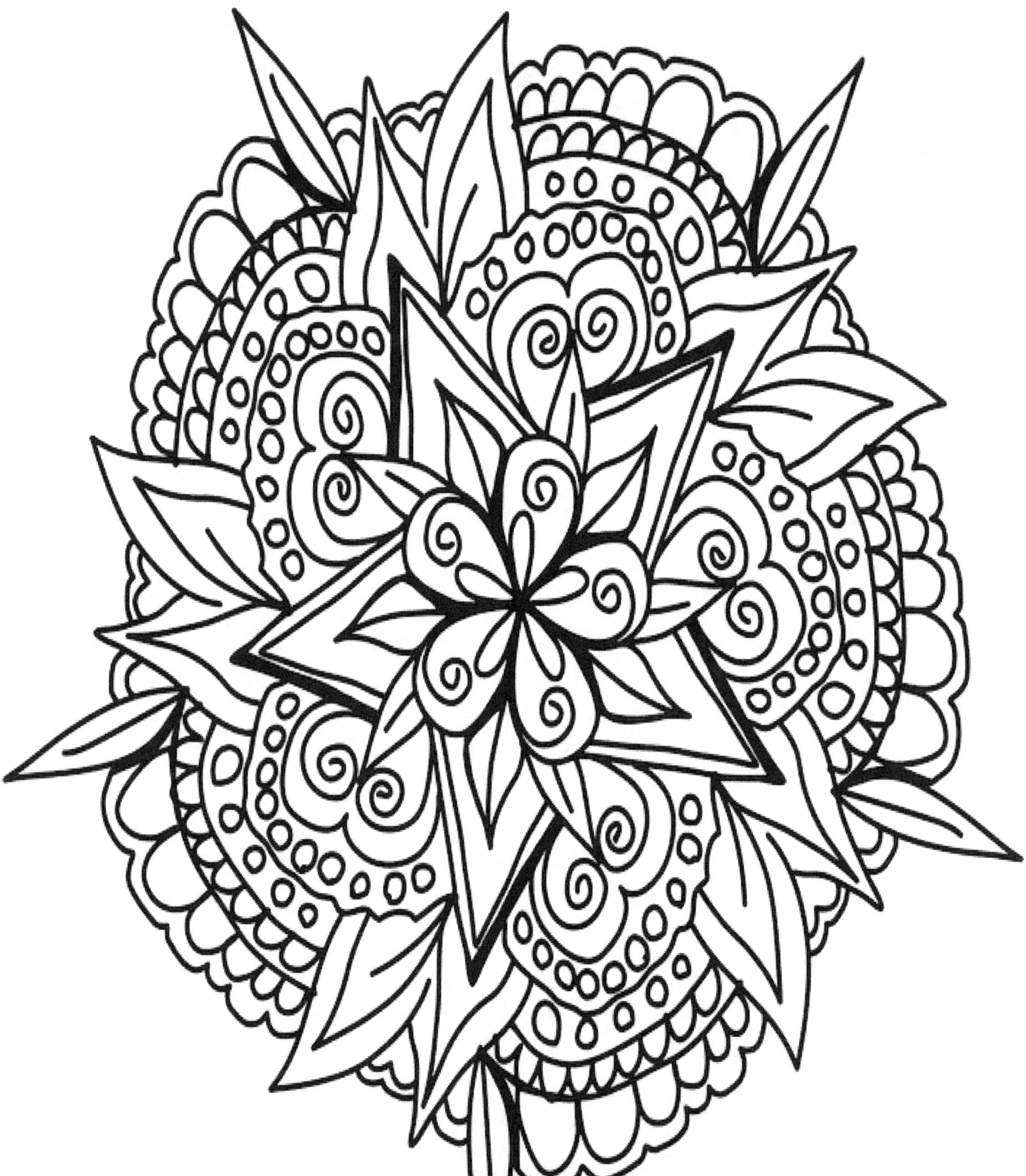

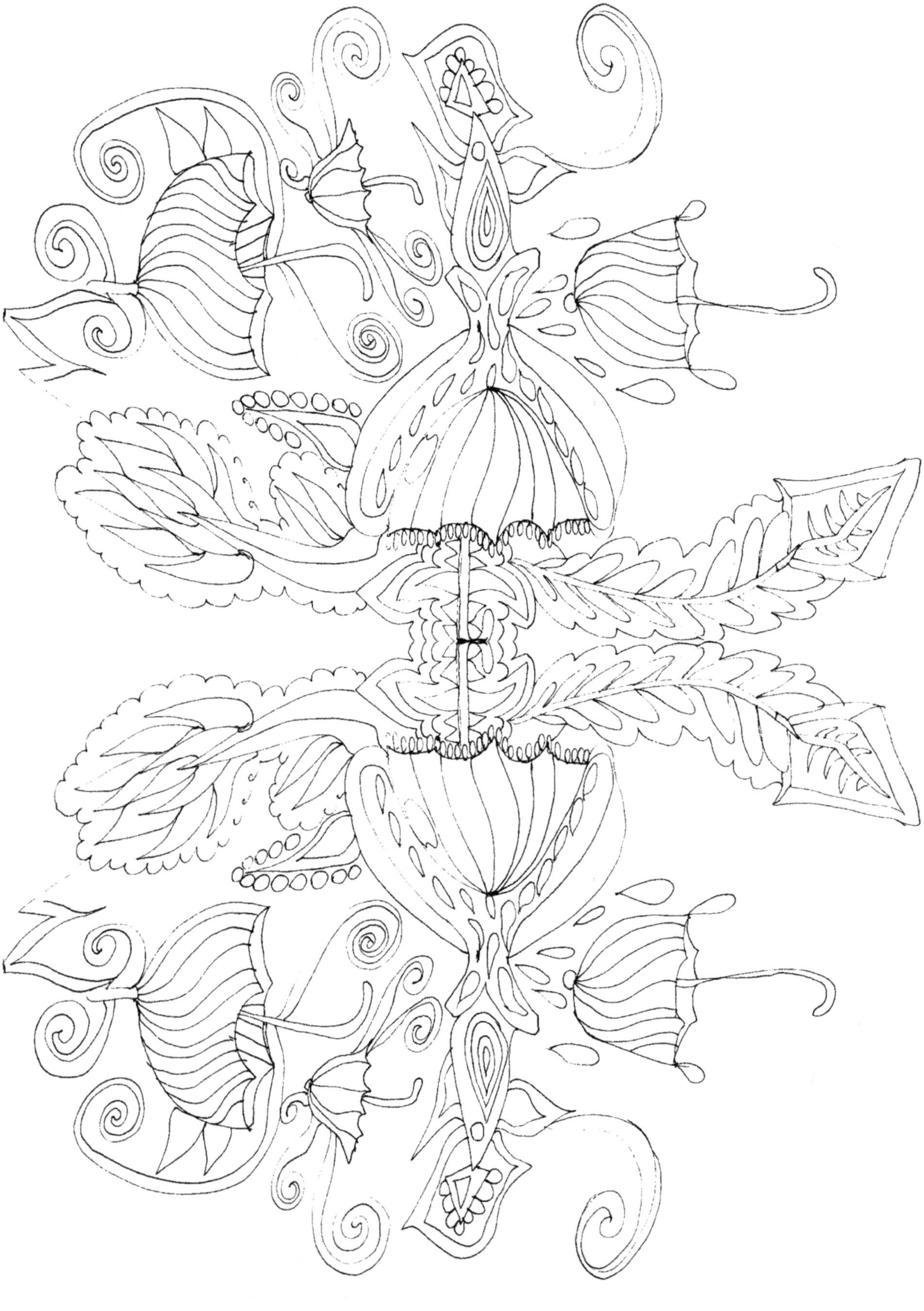

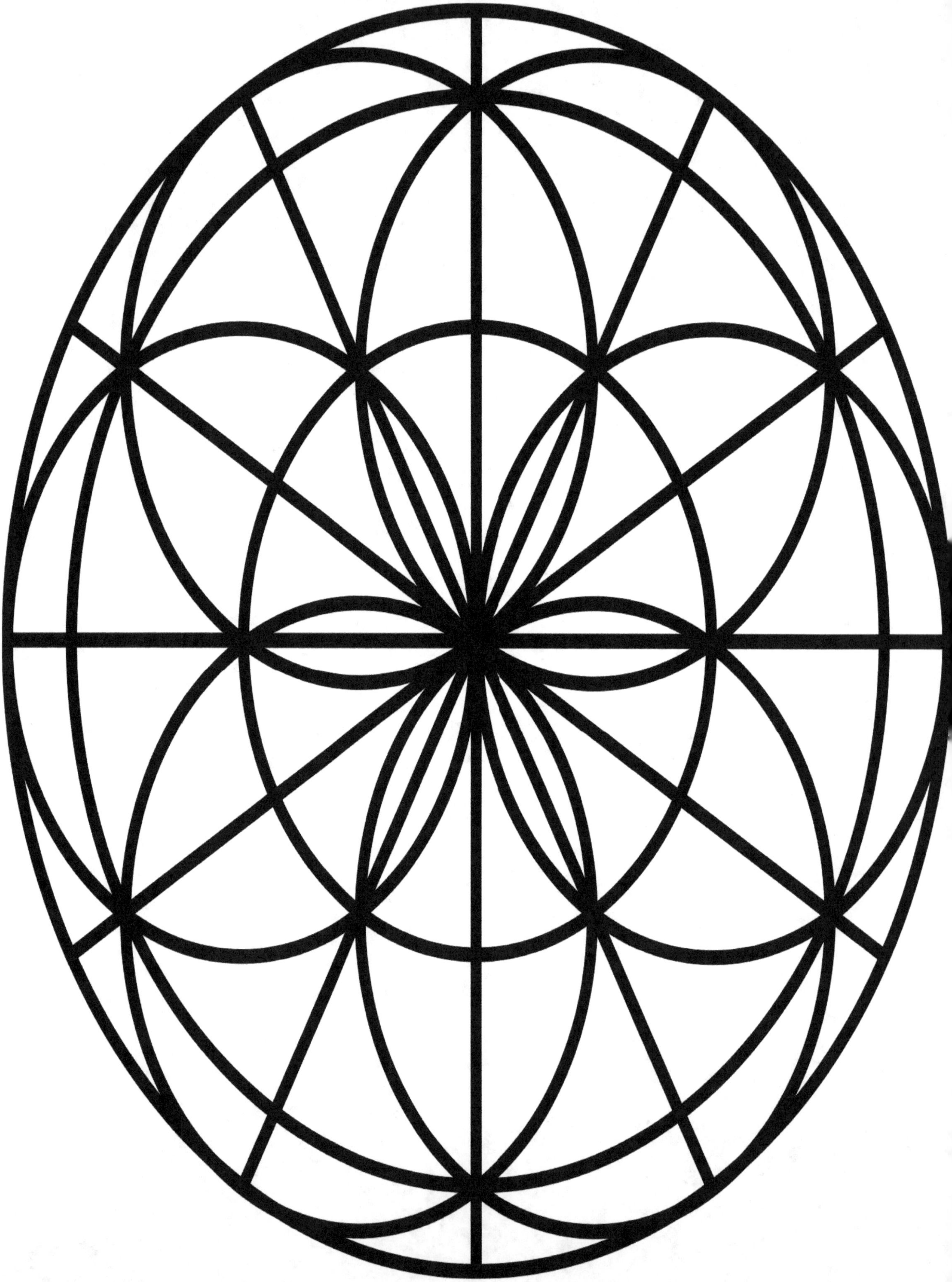

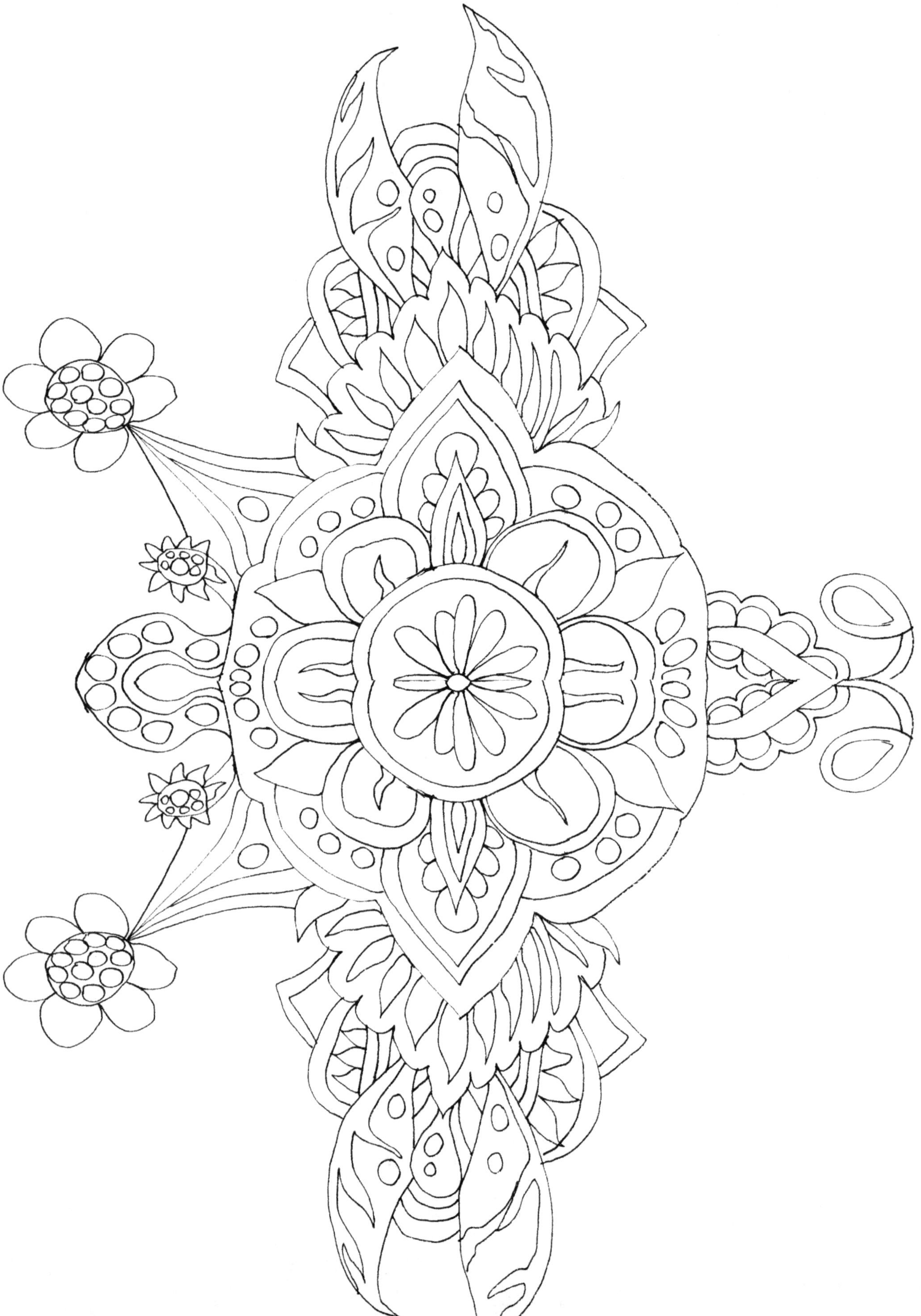

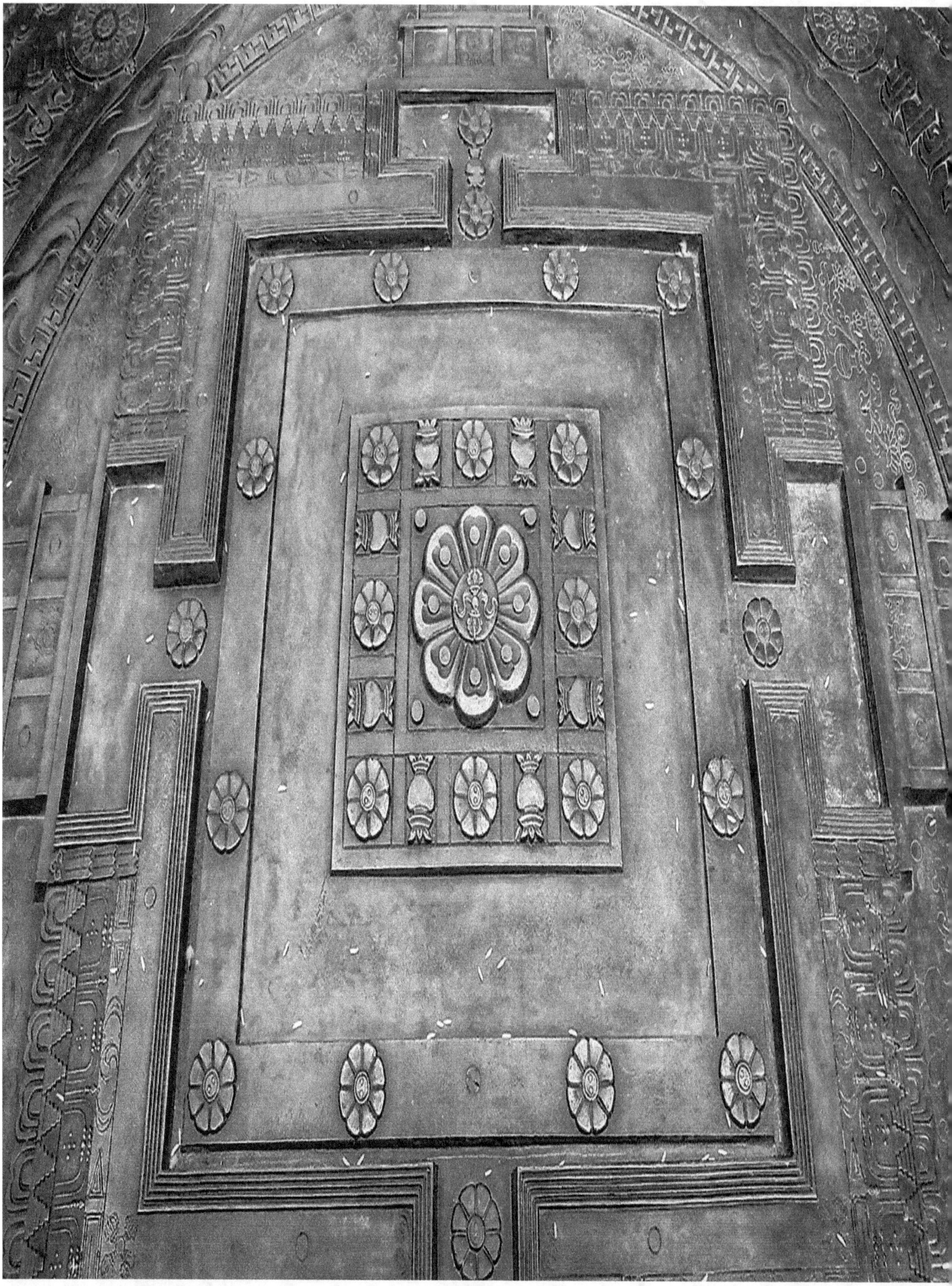

www.ingramcontent.com/pod-product-compliance
Lightning Source LLC
Chambersburg PA
CBHW060434220526
45465CB00008B/3136
* 9 7 9 8 6 0 7 9 0 3 0 7 7 *